THE FAMILY CREATIVE WORK SHOP

THE FAMILY CREATIVE WORKSHOP

19

Sundials, Supergraphics
Swedish Huck Work, Swings
Syrups, Table Games
Tables and Benches
Tablet and Frame Weaving
Tambour, Tatting

Plenary Publications International, Inc.
New York and Amsterdam

Published by Plenary Publications International, Incorporated 10 East 49th Street, New York, New York 10017, for the Blue Mountain Crafts Council.

Library of Congress Catalog Card Number: 73-89331.
Complete set International Standard Book Number: 0-88459-021-6.
Volume 19 International Standard Book Number: 0-88459-018-6.
Second Printing.

Manufactured in the United States of America. Printed and bound by the W.A. Krueger Company, Brookfield, Wisconsin.

Printing preparation by Lanman Lithoplate Company.

Publishers:
Plenary Publications
International, Incorporated
10 East 49th Street
New York, New York 10017

James Wagenvoord
EDITOR-IN-CHIEF

Jerry Curcio
PRODUCTION MANAGER

Peggy Anne Streep
VOLUME EDITOR

Joanne Delaney
EDITORIAL ASSISTANT

Editorial preparation:
Tree Communications, Inc.
250 Park Avenue South
New York, New York 10003

Rodney Friedman
EDITORIAL DIRECTOR

Ronald Gross
DESIGN DIRECTOR

Paul Levin
DIRECTOR OF PHOTOGRAPHY

Donal Dinwiddie
CONSULTING EDITOR

Jill Munves
TEXT EDITOR

Sonja Douglas
ART DIRECTOR

Rochelle Lapidus
Marsha Gold
DESIGNERS

Lucille O'Brien
EDITORIAL PRODUCTION

Ruth Forst Michel
COPYREADER

Eva Gold
ADMINISTRATIVE MANAGER

Editors for this volume:
Michael Donner
SUNDIALS
TABLES AND BENCHES

Linda Hetzer
SUPERGRAPHICS
SWEDISH HUCK WORK

Nancy Bruning Levine
SWINGS
TABLET AND FRAME WEAVING
TAMBOUR

Marilyn Nierenberg
TABLE GAMES

Mary Grace Skurka
SYRUPS
TATTING

Originating editor of the series:
Allen Davenport Bragdon

Contributing editors:
Sherry De Leon
Judy Pickett
Sid Sackson

Contributing photographers:
Paul Hogan
Bob Jones
Steve Kennerly
R. Newton Mayall
Steven Mays
Dr. Bruce M. Schlein

Contributing illustrators:
Marina Givotovsky
Patricia Lee
Lynn Matus
Sally Shimizu

Production:
Thom Augusta
Christopher Jones
Patricia Lee
Sylvia Sherwin
Leslie Strong
Gregory Wong

Photograph and Illustration credits:
SUNDIALS: Photograph, page 2314, Jantar Mantar observatory, courtesy of Information Service of India; drawing of Father Time, page 2320, by T. Erat Harrison. SUPER-GRAPHICS: Supergraphics, pages 2328 and 2335, photographed at Foremost Furniture, New York, New York. SWINGS: Woven adult swing, page 2354, courtesy of Spirit of the Earth Gallery, New Hope, Pennsylvania. SYRUPS: Soda fountain, page 2358, photographed at Albert's Coffee Shop, New York, New York. TAMBOUR: Painting, page 2406, courtesy of India Office Library, London, England; Indian crewel samples, page 2407, courtesy of Gurian Fabrics, Inc., New York; Turkish coverlet, page 2408 courtesy of Bernice Barsky, New York, New York; leafy pillow, page 2413, and blue cat wall hanging, page 2415, courtesy of Roxa Wright. TATTING: Balsa wood shuttle, pages 2424 and 2430, designed and constructed by Thom Augusta; handkerchiefs, left and center, page 2420, courtesy of Ruth Hetzer; right, courtesy of Helen Skurka; netting shuttle, page 2424, from School Products Company, Inc., New York, New York; antique tatting shuttles, page 2424, from the collections of Josephine Mayer and Audrey Hinkly.

The Project-Evaluation Symbols appearing in the title heading at the beginning of each project have these meanings:

Range of approximate cost:
¢ Low: under $5 or free and found natural materials

$ Medium: about $10

$$ High: above $15

Estimated time to completion for an unskilled adult:
⧖ Hours

🕐 Days

 Weeks

Suggested level of experience:
Child alone

Supervised child or family project

Unskilled adult

Specialized prior training

Tools and equipment:
Small hand tools

Large hand and household tools

Specialized or powered equipment

On the cover:
Yarn wrapped around a wooden shuttle passes over and under yarn stretched on a frame loom, forming the most basic weave, called the plain or tabby weave. See "Tablet and Frame Weaving," page 2392. Photograph by Paul Levin.

Contents and craftspeople for Volume 19:

SUNDIALS
Shadows of Times Past

R. Newton Mayall and Margaret W. Mayall are sundial experts; he is an engineer and she is an astronomer. Among their many published works are Sundials: How to Know, Use, and Make Them; The Sky Observer's Guide; *and* Skyshooting: Photography for Amateur Astronomers. *Mrs. Mayall was formerly the Pickering Memorial Astronomer at Harvard Observatory and Director of the American Association of Variable Star Observers. Mr. Mayall has designed and built nearly 100 sundials, many on public display.*

Reminders of a leisurely way of life that once existed, sundials are objects of nostalgic charm, fascinating the curious in this split-second era. It is hard to remember that they were once the universal clock. They were used well into the twentieth century, for example, to measure time for the French railroads.

Few people today would go to the trouble of making a sundial solely to tell time. It would be very difficult to make one that would compare in accuracy, say, with an inexpensive modern wristwatch, and even then the sundial would be harder to read and useless when the sun was not shining. Today, when clockwork governs transportation timetables, television programming, work and school hours, and many other things, the ancient time tellers have lost their authority.

Yet there is an abiding appeal in a clock that has no moving parts (except the earth itself), runs without being wound or needing a battery change, never needs repair, and measures time the way all nature does. Anyone who would like to make a sundial has an interesting do-it-yourself project in store. Any of the sundials described here would make a conversation-starting addition to a patio, yard, or clearing in the woods—and would serve as a clock on any sunny day of leisure as well.

The sundial was the commonest kind of clock until Britain's industrial revolution. Through the ages, innumerable types were devised. But all made equal use of a shadow (or ray of light) cast by the sun. What made the sundials work is the fact that the sun appears to travel across the sky in a predictable path at a predictable speed. Observation of its movements gave even early man a kind of clock. He must certainly have estimated where in the day he was by the length and direction of the shadows, if not by direct observation of the sun. So it was only a matter of time until a device was found to make such an estimate more formal and accurate.

But even today, basing a clock on the sun's movement is not simple. Many facts have to be taken into account. Three sundial projects of increasing sophistication are shown here. One (page 2313) is an adaptation of an ancient Egyptian crossbar sundial, devised about 1500 B.C. The second (page 2315) is a simplified dial requiring no arithmetical calculation. The third (page 2316) is an accurate horizontal dial for those who would like the challenge of a more advanced project. These sundials are among the easiest to understand and make. Unlike many others, which only work at certain times of the day and year, these can be used whenever the sun is shining. (If you wish to know more about sundials, there is a bibliography on page 2320.)

What Makes It Tick?

Before you make a sundial, picture what will make it work. Assuming you live north of the equator, you will experience the sun's daily and yearly motion more or

A South Carolina boy, Willy Schlein, takes an afternoon reading on a bowstring sundial at the Nathaniel Russell House in Old Charleston. This bronze sundial is calibrated at 5-minute intervals. Its dial face (the curved and numbered band) is parallel with the earth's equator. The gnomon, a shadow-casting bar, is parallel with the earth's axis and points to the North Celestial Pole (near the North Star), 33 degrees above Charleston's northern horizon.

A playful bronze sundial created by Brenda Putnam graces a walkway at the Brookgreen Gardens Museum of American Sculpture near Murrell's Inlet, South Carolina. As described on page 2316, you can make a simpler but equally functional sundial of painted wood for your own garden.

less as shown in Figure A. You are located in the center of the apparently flat disk, shown in green, whose edges represent the horizon you see every day. Four directions—north, south, east, and west—are indicated on the horizon line by their initials. In late June, when the sun travels through its highest and longest arc across the sky, it rises well to the north of east, passes high above you just south of the overhead point (the zenith), marked z, and sets well to the north of west. But in late December, when the sun travels its lowest and shortest path, it rises south of east, passes low above the southern horizon, and sets south of west. In late March and September, the sun is midway between these two extremes, rising exactly in the east and setting exactly in the west.

At any time of year, when the sun is at its high point for the day, it is noon, sun time, and your shadow will always point due north. But because at all other hours the sun's position varies with the seasons, the direction of a shadow at any hour other than noon will change gradually. This change has to be taken into account in some way to make a sundial accurate the year round.

This can be done, as the projects that follow demonstrate, but the makers of the earliest sundials dealt with these changes by expanding and contracting their concept of time to suit the seasons. In the subtropical regions where sundials were first used, the seasonal change is far smaller than in the temperate zone, so the differences were probably shrugged off, if not entirely overlooked. In addition, the 24-hour day was unheard of, and hours were not fixed in unvarying length. When people did divide daylight into 12 parts—perhaps the Babylonians of 2000 B.C.—the 12 hours did not represent periods of fixed duration. They were, rather, equal fractions of the total daylight on any given day. Thus, although the hours for any one day were equal, their length would vary with the duration of daylight. The first hour always began at sunrise, the seventh hour always began at noon, and the twelfth hour always ended at sunset. Intermediate hours on any one day began and ended at even intervals.

Such a system would provide the northern United States, for example, with daytime hours of up to 80 minutes in summer and a short 40 minutes in winter. Nights, as late as post-Roman times, did not consist of hours but of four quarters, called vigils. These were announced by the changing of night watchmen, whose tours of duty would vary (in northerly latitudes) from a pleasant 120 minutes in June to a bone-chilling 240 minutes in December. The use of 24 equal and unvarying hours became widespread with the introduction of mechanical clocks, which made them necessary as well as convenient.

Illusion or reality?

It will not be news to you that the apparent movement of the sun through the heavens is caused by the earth's movement on its axis while the sun stands still. With sundials, however, it is appearance that counts; so the explanation at right is based on the illusion of the sun's movement.

To simplify further, this explanation assumes you live in the northern hemisphere. If you live south of the equator, you will experience the sun's annual apparent movements in reverse order, insofar as north-south relationships are concerned, and your sundials will be mirror images of the ones shown here.

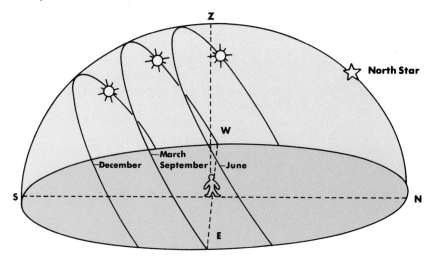

A

Figure A: A diagram of the dome of the northern hemisphere sky shows how the daily path of the sun varies at different times of the year. An observer stands in the center of an apparent disk formed by his horizon, shown in green and quartered by north-south and east-west lines. He sees the sun describe its most northerly arc in June and its most southerly arc in December. Only in March and September does the sun appear to rise directly to the east and set directly to the west. Except in the tropics, the sun never reaches the zenith directly overhead. At noon, the observer's shadow will always point due north, but at other times of day it will vary with the season, making the location of true north crucial for a sundial maker.

Environmental Projects
Amenhotep's clock

A crude sundial, based on the model invented in ancient Egypt (Figure B) and used by peasants to this day, can be made from two yardsticks and a scrap of wood. The upper yardstick casts a shadow on the lower one. Hour marks are set with the help of a watch and will change with the season of the year.

The earliest known sundial, made in Egypt around the time of Amenhotep (sixteenth century B.C.) was a simple crossbar like that shown in Figure B. Each morning, the crossbar on top was oriented along a north-south line, with the lower bar pointing west. The shadow of the upper bar (the gnomon) would fall on the lower bar (the dial face) and move across it as the day progressed. When the sun rose at the beginning of the first hour, the upper bar cast a nearly horizontal shadow extending beyond the end of the lower bar. The shadow reached the first mark on the lower bar at the beginning of the second hour (7 A.M. in late March). When it reached the next mark, the third hour began. Other points marked the beginning of the fourth, fifth, and sixth hours. When the crossbar ceased to cast a shadow, it was the seventh hour, noon. Then the lower bar had to be reversed so it pointed due east. The afternoon hours would then be registered in the reverse order of the morning hours. Marks occurred at irregular intervals, of course, because early morning and late afternoon shadows are extremely long and shadows around midday are relatively short. Most of the change in shadow length takes place early and late in the day.

No one really knows why the Egyptian who made this dial was content to change it every noon, when he could have simply extended the lower bar an equal distance past the base of the upright. This has been done in the yardstick sundial shown above.

To make this crude time-telling device, you will need two yardsticks (or comparable pieces of wood), a 2-inch length of dowel 1 inch or more in diameter (any 2-inch scrap of wood would do), and a few nails. The colors that mark the hours are optional. Center one of the yardsticks on the dowel, then drive two or three nails through the yardstick into the dowel. With a handsaw, cut a slot in the other end of the dowel at a right angle to the yardstick already attached, ½ inch deep and wide enough so the second yardstick slips into it on edge. Center the second yardstick in the slot. Balance it there; then secure it with two or three nails.

To use the yardstick sundial, place it on a level surface with the upper stick on a north-south line. You can establish this line by consulting a local newspaper for the

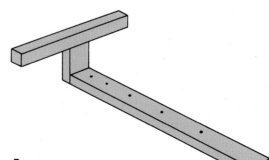

B

Figure B: Ancient Egyptian sundials had a raised crossbar set on a north-south line. A lower bar, the time indicator, faced west in the morning, but at noon it had to be reversed so it would point east. At each hour, the crossbar shadow passed a mark on the lower bar. (The noon turn is unnecessary if the lower bar projects both east and west, as pictured in the photograph above.)

day's sunrise and sunset times. At the moment of noon, precisely midway between sunrise and sunset, all shadows will point due north. (Do not use a compass; it is not accurate enough for a successful sundial.) When one hour has passed, clock time, mark the forward edge of the shadow on the lower yardstick; do the same after two, three, four, and five hours have passed. By the time six hours have passed, the shadow will most likely have passed beyond the end of the stick. Label the marks you have made 1, 2, 3, 4, and 5 o'clock respectively. Make corresponding marks for morning hours on the opposite end of the stick, so the 1 o'clock mark is the same distance from the center as the 11 o'clock mark, the 2 o'clock mark balances the 10, and so on. The result will be a symmetrical series of ten marks, labeled in sequence from 7 A.M. to 5 P.M. (The crossbar itself, when it casts no shadow, represents noon.)

If you like, you can paint the various hour zones different colors, or cover them with colored papers as pictured on page 2313.

These hour marks will be accurate only at the time of year when they were originally established. As the seasons change, the error will increase. You could make four such sundials, one for each season, to minimize the error. But if you make only one, the best time to do it is in late March or late September, when the sun is running on its middle course.

A remarkable open-air observatory in Jaipur, India, constructed of pink stucco between 1718 and 1734, has what are probably the largest sundials in the world. The shadow-casting gnomons contain stairways up to 118 feet in length, and their shadows—capable of unusually precise measurement because of the large scale—move at a rate of up to 2 inches per minute.

Environmental Projects
A child's portable sundial

The transition from primitive sundials to modern ones, though it consisted of a single, simple adjustment, was a long time in coming. A dial that could correct for the angle of the sun's rays at various seasons and at the same time register hours of fixed duration was not widely used in the West until the fourteenth century (though a Chinese model exists from the third century B.C.). This technological breakthrough consisted merely of tilting the gnomon's shadow-casting edge from its vertical position to an angle that would make it point to the North Celestial Pole from any particular latitude. This adjustment makes the sundial reliable the year round because the North Star lies near the line of the earth's axis, and it is around this axis that the sun appears to rotate every day of the year, regardless of its height in the sky. As the gnomon remains constantly at right angles to the sun, no seasonal adjustment is needed. Hour lines marked on the dial in June will still be accurate in December.

A further improvement occurred when someone discovered that if the dial face were tilted until it formed a right angle with the gnomon, the spacing of the hour lines would be greatly simplified. In fact, they fall at regular 15-degree intervals, like evenly spaced wheel spokes, rather than at irregular intervals.

A sundial with both gnomon and dial face tilted toward the North Celestial Pole is called an equatorial dial, because the dial face is exactly parallel to the earth's equator, which mirrors the sun's path in the sky.

The equatorial dial pictured, top right, was made from a translucent plastic-container lid 4 inches square and a pencil. To make it, punch a hole in the center of the lid just large enough for a pencil to fit snugly through it. Then inscribe the hour lines shown in the photograph an equal distance apart. To do this, draw the 6 o'clock lines squarely across the center of the hole, the noon line straight down from the hole, and extend the 9 A.M. and 3 P.M. lines diagonally from the hole to the lower corners of the lid. The placement of the intermediate hour lines can be judged by eye, with the 4, 5, 7, and 8 A.M. lines corresponding in direction to their P.M. counterparts. For a neat appearance, use 1/16-inch graphic tape, available at art supply stores, to cover the lines. Insert a sharpened pencil in the hole, point down.

Finding the Correct Angle
Set the sundial so the pencil eraser points to the North Celestial Pole, with the pencil perpendicular to the dial face. You won't have to do this by eye, for the angle the pencil point makes with the ground should be equal to the latitude of the place where you erect the dial. You can determine this angle by consulting a map. A child too young to read a map or to measure the angle with a protractor can use the table at the right. It tells how far you need to push the pencil through the hole to get the proper angle, depending on where you live and assuming you have used a 4-inch lid. (If your dial face is twice as large, double the distance shown in the table.)

Once the pencil is inserted to the proper depth, set the sundial in any level, sunny place, indoors or out, with the noon mark pointing down from the center hole and the pencil on a north-south line, its eraser end pointing north. (A way to find the true north-south line with shadows is given on page 2314.) If you use a soft base such as the earth, you can stabilize the dial by embedding the pencil point, but then you will have to pull the pencil that much farther through the hole in the dial face, or the angle will change.

There is one major drawback to many equatorial dials. Because the dial faces north and is parallel to the equator, shadows can be seen on the top surface only when the sun is in the northerly half of its annual course—from March to September in the northern hemisphere. In the other half of the year, a shadow is cast only on the bottom surface by the lower end of the pencil. If you use a translucent dial face, however, the shadow will still be discernible from above during the winter months, and you will not have to crane your neck to peer in at the lower face. For a few days in March and September, when the sun is on the same plane as the dial face, it will be difficult to see any shadow at all.

A sundial with reasonably good year-round accuracy can be made from a pencil and a plastic container lid. The pencil points to the North Star, and the dial surface parallels the equator and faces north. This arrangement permits the hour lines to be spaced equally.

Setting the portable sundial

If you live at or near the latitude of:	Push the pencil through the hole:
Mexico City Honolulu	5 inches
Miami	4½ inches
Jacksonville New Orleans Houston El Paso	4 inches
Atlanta Memphis Oklahoma City Albuquerque Phoenix Los Angeles	3½ inches
Boston New York Washington Chicago Denver San Francisco	3 inches
Halifax Quebec Montreal Toronto Minneapolis Portland	2½ inches
St. John's Winnipeg Great Falls Calgary Seattle	2 inches

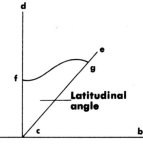

C

Figure C: To make a pattern for the shadow-casting gnomon of a sundial, draw two lines, the second perpendicular to the first (*a-b* and *c-d*). From their intersection, extend a line (*c-e*) at an angle to line *c-d* that is equal in degrees to the geographic latitude of the place where the sundial will be used. This line represents the gnomon's shadow-casting edge. Connect line *c-d* and line *c-e* with a line of any shape (*f-g*) to complete the gnomon outline. Just be sure line *c-f*, the gnomon's base, is of a size that will fit comfortably on the sundial face you are planning.

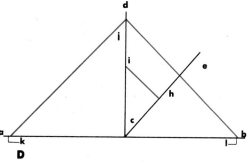

D

Figure D: Working with the gnomon drawing (Figure C), start making the sundial-face pattern by drawing a line (*h-i*) perpendicular to *c-e* and as far as *c-d*. Mark a point *j* on *c-d* so *i-j* is equal in length to *h-i*. Then mark points *k* and *l* on *a-b*, so *c-j* is equal in length to *c-k* and *c-l*. Draw lines connecting *j* with *k* and *l*.

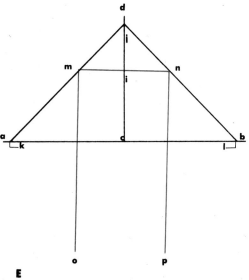

E

Figure E: Continue the dial-face pattern, started in Figure D, by drawing line *m-n* through point *i*, perpendicular to line *c-d*. Extend lines *m-o* and *n-p* past line *a-b*, parallel to line *c-d* and, of course, perpendicular to line *a-b*.

A horizontal sundial

A portable wooden sundial accurately tells the time (10:20 A.M.) in the Mayalls' Cambridge, Massachusetts, garden. You can make a sundial like this, or one of your own design, but you must adjust it to be accurate at the latitude where you live.

In recent centuries, the most popular sundial has been the horizontal variety, often ornamented and set on a pedestal in a garden. This type is more difficult to make than those in the preceding projects, but if you make it, you will have a reasonably accurate timepiece. Such an instrument must have a carefully measured dial face and shadow-casting gnomon, and the size and placement of these parts must have an exact relationship to each other. This relationship will vary, depending on the latitude of the place where you will use the sundial. Hence an all-purpose pattern cannot be made; you will need to work out the dimensions for your own particular location, as detailed below.

The Pattern
Before you commit your sundial design to permanent materials, work out the details on paper. Make the patterns for the gnomon and the dial face in a single drawing since their shapes must bear an exact relationship to each other. I use a drawing board, T square, drafting triangles, compass, and protractor, but the only tools you really need are a ruler and protractor.

Tape down a large sheet of graph paper, and draw a horizontal line across it, one-third of the way up from the bottom edge (line *a-b* in Figure C). From the middle of this line, extend a vertical line up to the top of the paper (line *c-d* in Figure C). Next, consult a reliable map to determine the latitude (within 1 degree) of the place where you will use the sundial. Placing the center of the protractor at point *c*, mark off in a clockwise direction from vertical line *c-d* the number of degrees equal to your latitude. Extend a line from point *c* through this mark (line *c-e* in Figure C). This is the crucial step of your pattern-making operation. Because the latitude of Cambridge, Massachusetts, where I live, is 42 degrees, my line *c-e* makes a 42-degree angle with line *c-d*. The lines forming this angle designate the two essential parts of the gnomon—line *c-d* is its base, and line *c-e* is its shadow-casting edge (called the style). The two lines may be any length, provided the gnomon fits on the dial face. Connect them with a third line (line *f-g* in Figure C), which may be straight, curved, or any fanciful form. This line is of no consequence in the operation of the sundial, only completing the outline of the gnomon.

Once the gnomon pattern is established, make the pattern for the horizontal sundial face on the same sheet of graph paper. You will use all the lines already drawn except line *f-g*. Line *a-c* represents the 6 A.M. line, *c-b* the 6 P.M. line, and *c-d* the noon line. These lines always form a perfect T, regardless of the latitude. The angles of the remaining hour lines, which will radiate like spokes from point *c*, are based on the latitude angle already established for the gnomon's style. From any point on line *c-e*, extend a perpendicular line as far as line *c-d*. This line is indicated as *h-i* in Figure D. Measure line *h-i*; then mark point *j* on line *c-d*, above point *i*, so *i-j* equals *h-i*. In like fashion, measure line *c-j*, and mark points *k* and *l* on line *a-b*, so *k-c* and *c-l* are both equal to *c-j*. Draw lines from point *j* to points *k* and *l*.

Next, draw a line through point *i* from line *j-k* to line *j-l*, perpendicular to line *c-d*. This line is marked *m-n* in Figure E. Draw lines *m-o* and *n-p* perpendicular to line *m-n*, down to the bottom of the paper.

With the center of the protractor at point *j*, mark points that are 15 and 30 degrees to either side of line *c-j* (photograph 1, page 2318). As shown in Figure F, extend lines toward all four marks from point *j*, stopping at line *m-n*. In the same way, set the center of the protractor at point *k*, and mark points that are 15 and 30 degrees to either side of line *k-c*. Extend lines toward these marks from point *k* as far as line *m-o*. Again, working from point *l*, draw four corresponding lines as far as line *n-p*.

From the points where these 12 lines meet the three-sided figure, *o-m-n-p*, draw lines to point *c* (Figure F). Also draw lines from points *m* and *n* to point *c*. These 14 lines, with the three hour lines drawn at the beginning, make up the 17 spokes of the standard sundial face. Number them in sequence, beginning with 4 A.M. at the lower left and moving clockwise to 8 P.M. at the lower right. This completes your sundial pattern.

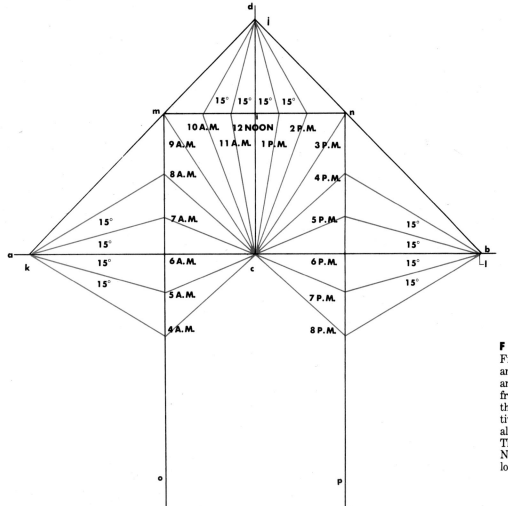

F

Figure F: From point *j* in Figure E, mark off angles 15 and 30 degrees to both sides of line *c-j* and extend lines as far as line *m-n*. Do the same from points *k* and *l*, relative to line *k-l*, extending the lines as far as line *m-o* and line *n-p*, respectively. Finally, draw lines connecting point *c* with all the line intersections on *m-o*, *m-n*, and *n-p*. These are the hour lines for your sundial face. Number them in clockwise order from 4 A.M. at lower left to 8 P.M. at lower right.

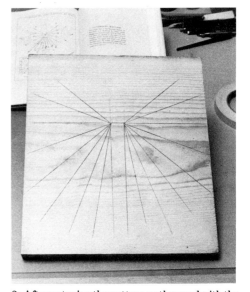

1: To measure and mark an angle, place the center of a protractor at the point where the angle will be formed (here, point *j*). Hold either the 90- or the 0-degree indicator on the existing line that will form one leg of the angle (here, line *c-j*). Mark the point along the protractor's edge that indicates the desired number of degrees in the angle or angles (in this case, 15 and 30). Then remove the protractor and draw the desired angles.

2: To mark the morning hour lines on the wood dial face, tape the tracing paper pattern to it with the central point *c* over point *y*, already marked on the wood as shown in Figure G, and the horizontal 6 o'clock lines on both paper and wood in alignment. Insert carbon paper and trace the 4 A. M. through 11 A. M. hour lines with a pencil, using a straightedge for accuracy.

3: After retaping the pattern on the wood with the central point over point *z* already marked on the wood (Figure G), mark the afternoon hour lines in the same way so you get this result. The lines need not be drawn to any particular length; only the angles they form are important. Later, lines can be extended or shortened to touch the border of your design.

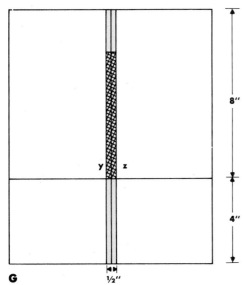

G

Figure G: In laying out the actual dial face, you will need to allow for a strip down the center that is the thickness of the gnomon (shown in blue). Where the gnomon will be attached is indicated by crosshatching. The 6 o'clock line (through points *y* and *z*) will be perpendicular to the gnomon zone (blue) crossing at the gnomon's tip. These lines should be marked on the dial face before the other hour markers are traced, as shown in photographs 2 and 3 (above).

The Materials

Garden sundials can be made of materials that range from stiff cardboard (for those kept indoors except during periods of observation) to cast bronze or stone. Old dials were usually engraved or etched in metal, and even today brass and aluminum sundials are common. Ceramic slabs, with incised or glazed hour marks, are popular in mild climates, but clay is hard to control when precise measurements are needed.

I have found you can make reasonably accurate and enduring sundials of painted wood, ½ to ¾ inch thick. The instructions that follow are for such a dial. A pedestal of wood, stone, concrete blocks, or other convenient material may be provided, or you can fasten the dial face securely to any existing level structure. Supports are discussed on page 2319.

The Dial Face

To make a ½-inch-thick, 10-by-12-inch sundial face with a 1-inch border, and a ½-inch-thick gnomon to match, you will need two smooth, unwarped pieces of wood, one 12 by 14 inches and the other 6 by 6 inches. Sand the dial face smooth, and give it two coats of white exterior paint. Before laying out the hour lines, take into account the thickness of the gnomon. If it were made of sheet metal or other thin material, no correction would be necessary, but because ½-inch wood is being used, the edge of the shadow will shift ½ inch to the right as the sun passes through the noon point. To solve this, just widen the noon line into a noon zone the thickness of the gnomon (shown in blue in Figure G). Then trace the morning and afternoon halves of the sundial separately, beginning in each case from the outer edge of the noon zone (photographs 2 and 3).

With a pencil, lightly draw a center line down the full length of the board's longer dimension (Figure G). Draw two more lines parallel to it, ¼ inch to either side. These represent the edges of the noon zone (and the gnomon). Across these lines, draw a perpendicular line one third of the way from the bottom edge of the board. This is the 6 o'clock line.

The base of the gnomon will be within the noon zone. The area it will occupy is shown in crosshatching in Figure G. Its forward tip (point *c* of Figure C, page 2316) will lie on the 6 o'clock line (*y-z* in Figure G). When you transfer the hour lines on the dial face, use point y of Figure G as the center from which the morning lines radiate, and point z as the center for the afternoon hours. In effect, you will be making two independent half-sundials, ½ inch apart, so you have one for each shadow-casting edge of the thick gnomon.

To fill in the hour lines, tape the pattern to the sundial face with the center point over point y (Figure G). Insert carbon paper and, with pencil and straightedge, transfer the morning hour lines onto the wood (photograph 2). Then shift the pattern so the center point is over point z (Figure G), and transfer the afternoon hour lines in the same way. The lines need not be drawn to the edge of the board; just make them long enough for the angles to be evident (photograph 3). Mark a 1-inch border around the board's edges with a pencil and straightedge, and you are ready to inscribe the design permanently on the wood. With a black indelible felt-tipped pen and a straightedge, ink in the border and extend the hour lines from the center points to the border. Number the hours in Roman or Arabic numerals, either in the border area or next to the lines. There are now two noon lines, one on either edge of the noon zone. Color the pattern thus formed with colored paints or wood stains, or, if you prefer, simply varnish the wood to protect it and to keep the lines and numbers from weathering.

The Gnomon
Trace the gnomon pattern onto the 6-inch wood square, and saw out the shape. A curved back edge can be cut with a jigsaw or fretsaw. Sand the gnomon lightly, and finish it as you did the dial face. When the gnomon is dry, nail it to the dial face in the noon zone with the end of its shadow-casting edge straddling points y and z of Figure G. Waterproof white glue and 2-penny brads will fasten the gnomon securely to the dial, but check with a drafting triangle or try square to make sure the gnomon is perpendicular to the base.

Mounting the Dial
For your sundial, choose the location that has the greatest exposure to the sun at all times of the day and year. Avoid areas near high trees or buildings. Sundials do not have to be permanently mounted. The one shown on page 2316 is portable. When I want to take a reading from it, I simply align the gnomon with a north-south line I have marked on a flat, level, patio flagstone.

But if you want a permanent base, a pedestal or other support can be used. A discarded table leg, a tree stump, the top of a low wall or handrail, or a birdbath stand would do, so long as it is an appropriate height (up to 4 feet) and has a level top. Use nails or screws and glue to join the dial to a base, or set the dial in a bed of mortar to attach it to a stone or masonry base. In either case, be sure the noon mark lies along a true north-south line, and the dial face is level in both directions (north-south and east-west).

You can determine an accurate geographic north-south line in a number of ways. The method described on page 2314 is perhaps the simplest. If you can determine your exact location with respect to landmarks on your visible horizon, you can use a detailed area map to establish a north-south line. The North Star (see Figure H), which is never more than 1¼ degrees from true north, is also reliable (despite this small inaccuracy), especially if you can align your sighting of it with a true vertical such as a plumb line suspended from a tree branch. Finally, a fitting method is to measure the length of a shadow cast by the sun. To do this, push a stick vertically in the ground, and mark the end of its shadow with a pebble every five minutes or so, beginning late in the morning and ending when you are certain the shadow has begun to lengthen again. A line drawn from the stick to the pebble that marks the shortest shadow is a true south-to-north line. (The shortest shadow may not be noon, local time, but where sundials are concerned, it is the sun, and not the church bell or the noon whistle, that must be believed.)

Reading the Sundial
Reading the sundial is simple enough. Just note the position of the edge of the gnomon's shadow in relation to the hour lines on the dial face. When the shadow's edge is precisely on a line, it is the hour indicated by that line. When it falls midway between two lines, it is half past the earlier of the two hours. Quarter hours and even smaller time intervals can be estimated fairly accurately by eye.

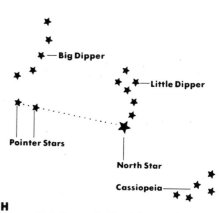

H
Figure H: To locate the North Star (and thereby establish a nearly true geographical north-south line for your sundial), extend an imaginary line from the pointer stars of the Big Dipper (the two outer stars of its cup). If the Big Dipper eludes you, look for it opposite, W-shaped Cassiopeia, an equal distance on the other side of the North Star.

Where space limitations do not permit a horizontal sundial, a vertical dial fastened to a wall is a good alternative. Easy to read but limited to the hours when the sun shines on the wall, this wrought-iron dial is mounted on a New York townhouse. The gnomon points south from the top of the dial face and protrudes at an angle equal to 90 degrees minus the latitude. The sun, filtered through tree foliage, casts a soft shadow beneath the gnomon just to the left of the noon mark.

Correcting an erratic sun

Even the most accurate of sundials will be a few minutes off at certain times due to cyclical fluctuation in the sun's passage through the dome of the sky. To take a reading accurate within two minutes, make these adjustments:

Period of the year	Adjustment
January 1-10	Add 5 minutes
January 11-26	Add 10 minutes
January 27-March 1	Add 15 minutes
March 2-20	Add 10 minutes
March 21-April 6	Add 5 minutes
April 7-28	No adjustment
April 29-May 31	Subtract 5 minutes
June 1-25	No adjustment
June 26-August 24	Add 5 minutes
August 25-September 9	No adjustment
September 10-23	Subtract 5 minutes
September 24-October 9	Subtract 10 minutes
October 10-November 27	Subtract 15 minutes
November 28-December 9	Subtract 10 minutes
December 10-20	Subtract 5 minutes
December 21-31	No adjustment

An allegorical personification of time has the traditional wings, scythe, and hourglass and is at once youthful and aged. The Latin emblem on this nineteenth-century engraving means "The end crowns the work."

For further reading

A Choice of Sundials, by W.W. Dolan, The Stephen Greene Press, Brattleboro, Vt., 1975.
Sundials, by F.W. Cousins, Pica Press, New York, New York, 1970.
Sundials, by R.K. Marshall, Macmillan Co., New York, 1963.
Sun-dials and Roses of Yesterday, by A.M. Earle, Charles E. Tuttle Co., Rutland, Vt., 1971.
Sundials: How to Know, Use, and Make Them, by R.N. and M.W. Mayall, Sky Publishing Corp., Cambridge, Mass., 1973.
Sundials, Their Theory and Construction, by A.E. Waugh, Dover Publications Inc., New York, New York, 1973.

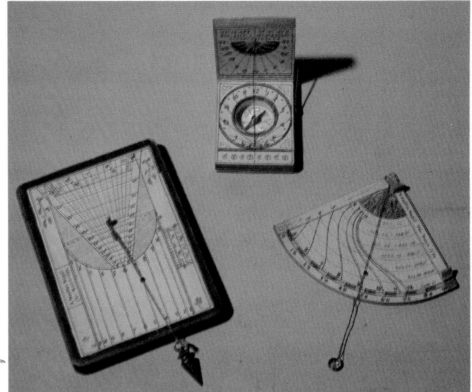

There are many ways that the sun's shadow can be used to tell time, and the various instruments devised to do this are bewildering at first glance. Three portable sundials made by R. Newton Mayall in 1939 are, left to right: a universal dial, which has a specially knotted and weighted shadow-casting thread so it can be used at any latitude; a folding pocket dial, which includes a compass that can be adjusted to the magnetic variation from true north before each reading; and a dial with curved hour lines that automatically adjust the reading for the time of year when it is taken.

Having taken your first reading, compare it with the time indicated by a reliable clock. Your sundial reading may vary from local civil time by anywhere from a few minutes to as much as 2 hours and 15 minutes. If you have not made an error in your calculations or measurements, the difference will be due to something that can be compensated for by simple arithmetic, as described below.

Standard Time

One factor is the variation between local and standard time. A century ago, each locality determined its time by the passage of the noonday sun overhead. For every degree of longitude that separated two towns, there was a four-minute difference in time. When it was noon in Philadelphia, located at a longitude of 75 degrees west, it was 12:04 P.M. in New York, which lies one degree to the east, and 11:52 A.M. in Washington, D.C., two degrees to the west. (This is the kind of time that sundials register.)

When it became necessary to standardize time, a system was worked out whereby time would be determined by the longitude at a central location in a region. The continental United States was divided into four such regions, known today as the Eastern, Central, Mountain, and Pacific time zones, and the standard time for those regions was established by the time at 75, 90, 105, and 120 degrees west longitude. To adjust sundial time to standard time, determine your longitude to within 1 degree of accuracy. Compare it to the standard meridian listed above for your time zone. If the two are the same, no adjustment is necessary. If you are east of the standard meridian (that is, if your longitude has a lower number) subtract four times that numerical difference, in minutes, from every sundial reading you take. If you live west of the standard meridian (at a longitude of a higher number) add four times the difference. The adjustment is usually a small one and can often, but not always, be ignored. (Some people living in the upper peninsula of Michigan have to add a full hour to their sundial readings to convert to standard time.)

This elegant sundial of bronze and marble serves as a reminder to choose a motto wisely. Erected in New York's Central Park in 1932, it bears the foolhardy Latin inscription *Ne dirvatvr fvga temporvm*, which means, loosely, "May it never be destroyed by time's flight." That did not stop vandals from chipping away the marble and defacing it with graffiti.

The Equation of Time

A second factor in adjusting your sundial reading is correcting for the sun's cyclical fluctuation from its average course. When accurate mechanical clocks were invented, it was learned that the sun appears to speed up and slow down slightly by a few seconds each day at different times of the year. In the course of a year, this difference accumulates to as much as 16 minutes before the cycle reverses itself and balance is restored. Because it would be inconvenient to make some days longer than others, timekeepers use only the average day, 24 hours, between noon points.

But sundials, with allegiance only to the sun, do not compensate for this cyclical fluctuation. You can correct for it if you like. For year-round accuracy within seven minutes, add 10 minutes to your reading in January, February, and March, and subtract 10 minutes from mid-September to mid-December. For an accuracy of within two minutes, find the date in the table (top left, opposite), and make the adjustment indicated next to it.

Daylight Saving Time

The third factor in adjusting your sundial reading is the most simple and obvious one—correcting for daylight saving time when it is in effect. In this case, you just add one hour to your adjusted sundial reading.

Mottos and Decorations

Some people like to decorate a sundial with a pictorial motif or a pithy bit of philosophy. A common design on sundial faces is the sun itself, centered on the dial face, with the spokelike hour lines as its rays. Allegorical representations of Time, such as the one pictured opposite, and stylized personifications of the Four Seasons, are other popular themes.

For related entries, see "Astronomy," "Birds and Birdhouses," "Maps and Pathfinding," "Time Telling," and "Weather Forecasting."

Sundial inscriptions

Serene I stand amyddst ye flowres
To tell ye passing of ye houres.

Dost thou love life?
Then do not squander time,
For time is the stuff that life is made of.

I am a shadow.
So art thou.
I mark time.
Dost thou?

Time and tide tarry for no man.

Biblical quotations have been a common inspiration:

Our days on earth are as a shadow,
and there is none abiding.
—Chronicles 1:29, 15

Let there be light:
and there was light.
—Genesis 1:3

Man is like to vanity:
his days are as a shadow
that passeth away.
—Psalms 144:4

Remember how short my time is.
—Psalms 89:47

Truly the light is sweet and a pleasant thing it is for the eyes to behold the sun.
—Ecclesiastes 11:7

Latin mottoes lend an antiquarian air:

Tempus fugit. (Time flies.)

Sol est lux et gloria mundi.
(The sun is the light and glory of the world.)

Sic transit gloria mundi.
(Thus passes the glory of the world.)

Sic transimus omnes. (Thus pass we all.)

Some literary references are appropriate also:

Thou by the dial's shady stealth may know
Time's thievish progress to eternity.
—Shakespeare

None can call again the passed time.
—Spencer

For tho' we sleep, or wake, or roam, or ride,
Ay fleeth the time, it will no man abide.
—Chaucer

Time flies.
Lines rise and shadows fall.
Let it pass by.
Love reigns forever over all.
—Quarles

Time goes, you say? Ah, no!
Alas, time stays, we go!
—Ronsard

Tyme passeth and speaketh not.
Deth cometh and warneth not.
Amende today and slack not.
Tomorrow thyself cannot.
—Anonymous

SUPERGRAPHICS

The Big Picture

A supergraphic is a bright, bold design painted onto a large surface such as a wall or ceiling. It can be used simply for decoration (it is less expensive than wallpaper). Or it can be used to achieve a particular effect—to define an area, to connect objects in a room visually, to make a tall ceiling look lower or a low one look higher, or to frame something such as a sofa or a window.

The design of a supergraphic is composed of two elements, color and line. The colors you use will probably be determined by the color scheme that exists in the room, but there are some guidelines to consider. Deep or warm colors such as red and yellow seem to advance, making a space seem smaller, more than pale or cool colors such as blue and green. What a color looks like can be affected by the color next to it; so experiment on paper first. Use colored felt-tipped markers, or cut out pieces of construction paper. Spend some time with the color scheme for any graphic before you commit yourself to it by painting it on the wall. Remember that a supergraphic can be painted in several shades of one color or in colors completely different from those in the rest of the room.

Once you have selected colors, you will have to develop a design that works. To develop a design, draw the wall or walls on paper and to scale, including permanent features such as windows, doors, and large pieces of furniture. You can use the design to accent architectural features or to disguise architectural flaws that you don't want emphasized. A closet door in the middle of a wall, for example, can be camouflaged by having the design go across the door instead of around it. As with color, decide what you are going to do on paper before you attempt anything on the wall. There will usually be an opportunity for some improvisation when you put the design on the wall, but having worked it out on paper reduces the chance of error.

Preparing the Wall

Before you paint a supergraphic on the wall, give the wall a fresh coat of interior wall paint—allowing a full drying interval before applying the graphic. Use low-luster or eggshell-finish latex enamel wall paint for both the base coat and the graphic itself. Semigloss latex can be used instead, especially if you are painting walls in a bathroom or kitchen that will require periodic washing. Latex flat wall paint is sometimes used, but it is not as durable as low-luster or semigloss latex paint. High-gloss latex is difficult to work with; it does not go on evenly and every brushstroke shows. A wall painted with high-gloss paint shines when viewed at any angle except straight on, which can destroy the effect of the supergraphic.

If your wall has already been painted with an oil or alkyd paint, you should use oil or alkyd paint for the graphic because latex paint does not adhere properly over oil. If you want to switch to latex, you can cover just the design area of the wall with a shellac-based, alcohol-soluble primer. This primer coat dries quickly; you do not have to wait more than an hour before starting your graphic.

If your graphic is in an area where it will be subjected to a lot of wear and tear, as in a hall or a child's room, you can increase its durability with a top coat of vinyl or latex varnish. Dilute the varnish with water (never use it straight). Such water-based varnish will give a high gloss to the graphic; so experiment with the amount of dilution to see how much gloss you want. The varnish can be applied with a roller after the supergraphic paint is dry; it will darken the colors slightly. Low-luster latex is quite durable; so this top coat is needed only for extra protection.

To apply the paint in the graphic, I depend on a 3½-by-5½-inch foam-backed mohair-faced pad. Such pads can be ordered from mail-order catalogs. When you apply paint with such a pad, always stroke in the same direction. Avoid stroking backward. The nap of the mohair pad is directional; it should point away from the direction you are stroking. Avoid overloading the pad with paint. Too much paint is

Ed Seymour was an advertising writer and executive for various publishing houses before he started painting supergraphics. He created one for his own home in Glen Ridge, New Jersey, and soon started a new career for himself. Ed has created a wide range of graphic designs for shops, stores, and offices, as well as homes, throughout the metropolitan New York area.

A cheerful note for a child's room is this stylized sun rising over rolling green hills. Details of how this supergraphic was painted can be found on page 2330.

difficult to control. In addition to the pad, you will need: shallow disposable aluminum pans to hold the paint; masking tape; polymer matte medium (available at art supply stores) to seal the tape; and two nylon artist's brushes.

After you apply the fresh latex base coat, wait at least overnight before painting the graphic, especially if you are going to use masking tape. If humidity is high, wait 48 hours. When the base coat is not completely dry, the masking tape tends to pull this paint off. Reserve some extra base coat paint for touching up if this happens and to cover slight mistakes and visible pencil lines. Do not put tape over any area—graphic or base paint—that is not thoroughly dry. With a little care, you can paint freehand along any newly painted edge that can't be taped.

If you make a mistake or miss a spot, do not try to touch it up while the paint is partially dry. Wait until you are ready to apply the second coat after the first coat has dried overnight. You almost always need two coats of paint to achieve an even layer of color. If your design abuts the ceiling, floor, or a corner, do not paint all the way into the angle or you might get paint on the adjacent surface. Instead, end the design ⅛ or ¼ inch from the angle. Have a wet rag on hand. If you paint beyond your end line, you can remove the excess paint if you wipe it away quickly. If you decide to make a large change, wait a day until the paint has dried; then sand down the paint with fine sandpaper. Cover it with one or two coats of the base paint, letting each coat dry. Although the base color might cover the graphic color, without sanding, the edge thickness of the layer of paint beneath will show through.

Paint and Color
Geometric supergraphic $ ● ♦ 🎨

When you have worked out a design on paper, you need to transfer it to the surfaces to be painted. At this stage you will need: a pencil; a kneadable eraser (it scuffs wall paint the least); a piece of string that will not stretch; a yardstick; a carpenter's level; and a carpenter's plumb line with chalk if you are making a long horizontal. If a circle is to be part of your design, draw the circle first; it becomes the focus around which the design works. In case you want to change the design slightly, horizontal or vertical stripes are easier to move than circles.

Before putting a circle on the wall, determine the visual center of the design. This can be wherever you want it to be, depending on the furniture in the room, its architectural features, and the area where you want the eye to be drawn. Tie the string to a pencil to make a compass. Hold the string tautly in the center of the circle with one thumb while you draw the circle, if the circumference is within reach (photograph 1). Make a pencil dot at the center of the circle so you can relocate it later. To make a larger circle, tape the string to the center point (photograph 2).

To ensure a straight, true line when you draw horizontals, place a yardstick on top of a carpenter's level (photograph 3, page 2326). If the level has two-way bubbles, you can also use it with a yardstick to draw the vertical lines (photograph 4). From most angles, a vertical stripe will look narrower than a horizontal stripe of the same width. So add 1 or 2 inches to the width of vertical stripes when you want them to look the same width as horizontal stripes. To soften the square corners of right-angle bends, draw an arc using the width of the horizontal stripe as the radius (photograph 5). Or you can experiment, starting with a larger radius and making progressively smaller arcs to get sharper corners.

To draw a long, uninterrupted horizontal line, a carpenter's plumb line is more convenient than a yardstick and level. If the floor (or ceiling) is level, measure from it to get two end points. Tape one end of the chalked plumb line at one of the marks, and hold the line over the other mark. Stretch the line to make sure it is level. With your free hand, pull the line away from the wall and let it snap back (photograph 6). It will leave a long, straight line of chalk. You can use the chalked plumb line to make long vertical lines, too. If the line has a plumb bob (or any weight) at the bottom end, it will automatically rest at true vertical.

When all the design lines are penciled on the wall, you are ready to put masking tape along the edges of the stripes you will paint. (It is difficult to make masking tape follow curves; it is easier to paint them freehand.) Make sure the tape lies just

1: To make a small circle with a string-and-pencil compass, hold the string at the center of the circle with one thumb and draw the circle with the other hand, keeping the string taut.

2: To draw a circle with a radius larger than you can comfortably reach, tape the string to the wall at the center point and draw the circle, keeping the string taut.

outside the pencil and chalk lines (photograph 7), and press it down. Seal this tape by brushing clear polymer matte medium over the edge so no paint can creep under the tape (photograph 8). When this quickly dries, you are ready to paint.

Before you start to paint, spread newspapers or an inexpensive paper or plastic dropcloth on the floor and arrange your equipment, including the latex paint, paint pads, shallow aluminum foil trays, artist's brushes, and damp rag. Decide the order of colors to be applied—interrupted lines and top lines should be painted first; continuous or bottom lines should be painted last. Pour the first paint into a shallow tray. Dampen the paint pad slightly, and run your hand along the pad to determine the way the nap runs. Then dip the pad into the paint so the working edge has paint on it. Wipe off the excess on the lip of the tray (photograph 9). When painting, always stroke with the nap of the pad, not against it.

Apply the paint in the areas edged with tape. Any long straight edge should be taped to ensure neatness. When you come to untaped curves, the flat pad allows you to follow the contours of your design quite easily. To go around a curve, follow the arc with the natural swing of your wrist or arm (photograph 10). Used with care, the paint pad gives clean, crisp edges. Use this same movement for the larger arcs of the circles (photograph 11). When you must end a stripe, as when a stripe of another color will intersect it, tape across the stripe being terminated. Seal it; then paint onto the tape (photograph 12). This way you avoid having to paint into a point. If a stripe in your design ends on one wall rather than being carried over to an adjacent wall, simply cutting it off straight across may seem too abrupt. Instead, slant the end (photograph 13). The degree of the slant will depend on the rest of your design. Tape the slanted edge, and use the paint pad in a continuous stroke over the edge onto the tape. When the area is fairly dry (wait at least one hour), you can carefully pull off the tape and have a straight edge of paint (photograph 14).

A conventional room with windows in one wall (to the right) is given a focal point with a circular supergraphic. The color scheme is subtle—just three shades of brown—so the drama would be concentrated in the size of the design. It almost completely covers one wall of the room and extends onto an adjacent wall.

3: To draw a perfectly straight horizontal line that does not waver, use a yardstick balanced on top of a carpenter's level, making sure the bubble is centered between its marks.

4: If your level has two bubbles, the second set in a tube mounted crosswise, you can use it with a yardstick to make sure that the vertical lines are perfectly true.

5: To soften the corners where horizontal and vertical lines meet, use a string-and-pencil compass to draw a curve. I used the width of the horizontal stripe as the radius of the curve.

6: To make a long horizontal line, tape one end of a plumb line at the desired height. Stretch the line to another marked point. Then snap the line against the wall so it leaves a line of chalk dust.

7: Put masking tape along the edges of the stripe you are going to paint, making sure the tape adjoins the pencil lines exactly. Make sure the tape is outside the stripe to be painted.

8: To make sure no paint will leak under the masking tape (giving you a ragged edge), first seal the inner tape edge carefully with colorless polymer medium. This step is time well spent.

9: Dip the mohair pad into the paint tray so that only the outer half has paint on it. Wipe off excess paint on the lip of the tray. Too much paint is difficult to control.

10: To paint a curved arc, follow the penciled line freehand with the natural swing of your wrist. This will give you a smoother edge than you can get if you try to tape the edge of a curve.

11: The natural movement of your entire arm, as you follow the carefully penciled line, will let you paint larger arcs and circles without the help of taped edges.

12: To end a stripe with a right angle, put tape across the design at the cut-off point. Then paint onto the tape, being careful not to cross it. This way you don't have to paint into the angle.

13: Often you will want to end a stripe on a slant so it does not terminate too abruptly. Again, tape the angle you want; then paint a bit onto the tape. This lets you avoid having to paint a point.

14: When the paint is dry to the touch (wait at least one hour), slowly pull off the masking tape. It will leave a clean, sharp edge of paint against the white background.

A simple blue-and-yellow color scheme is used in massive areas in this supergraphic covering most of the wall space in a child's bedroom. The stripes are continuous around all four walls of the room matching the width of window shutter and valance. The focal point of the supergraphic is a large yellow circle; the blue and yellow stripes dip under it.

Paint and Color
A child's room

$ ● ♪ ⚙

The geometric elements described in the preceding project were also used to decorate the child's bedroom shown above. The color scheme of bright yellow and two shades of blue with white gives the room a cheerful feeling. The inspiration for this design came from the window treatment. The two shades of blue that existed in the valance (the fabric-covered box across the top of the window) and in the shutter were repeated in the blue stripes of the supergraphic. The cheerful yellow was added to complete the color scheme. Yellow accessories were added to the room after the graphic was completed.

The yellow circle (shown above, right), off-center on its wall, is the center of the design, and the stripes continue all around the room. The lighter blue stripe is the width of the valance; the darker blue stripe is the width of the shutters.

Paint and Color
Framing furniture

$ ● ♪ ⚙

The supergraphic design shown at the top of page 2328, contained on one wall, echoes the shape of the sofa below and provides a dramatic frame for it. The lines of the supergraphic echo and emphasize the straight, sleek lines of the modern sofa so together they give the room a strong focal point. The black rectangle, centered above the sofa, emphasizes the geometric angularity of the contemporary furnishings. Brown and rust-colored stripes, colors repeated elsewhere in the room, form a ribbonlike pattern by overlapping each other and the black rectangle. Notice that these stripes end with a diagonal slant. Although the theme of this design is angular, the stripes are given a fluid look by rounding the corners. The use of black and two shades of brown adds a sophisticated note to the design.

To make this design or one similar to it, determine the size and placement of the rectangle first. (In the design pictured, the rectangle is above eye level.) Then work with small colored strips of paper until you are pleased with the pattern.

The supergraphic and the sofa together create a single focal point—and a strong one—in this living room. The painted design echoes the shape, color, and sophistication of the contemporary furnishings in the room.

Paint and Color
A dark background

Using a strong color as the background and white as one of the design colors gives a different look to a supergraphic. In the example below, bright red becomes the background color for a supergraphic on one wall of a child's bedroom. If you decide to use such a strong color as background, paint the graphic design first with white or tinted primer and let it dry (it dries quickly). Then apply the finishing colors of the graphic. This keeps the background from showing through.

This graphic, although heavily weighted on the red wall, continues onto the window wall to the right in the photograph. The window wall is white, as are other walls in the room. Where the white line in the graphic turns the corner, the line changes to red. The navy blue ring on the red wall is repeated as a smaller blue circle between two windows to the right of the photograph (not pictured).

A stunning effect is achieved by using a bright design color as a background color on one wall. The white that is the wall color elsewhere becomes a design color here. The white stripe changes to red when the supergraphic turns the corner onto the white wall at the right.

Paint and Color
Positive and negative

A positive-negative effect on adjacent walls can be achieved by reversing the colors at the corner, as shown below. The design pictured is very simple, combining a ringed half-circle with horizontal lines. The strength of the design lies in the change of colors. To achieve balance, the shorter wall was painted so the dark colors (brown and green) dominate. The longer wall seems lighter because the background color is white. The corner graphic frames the modular sofa that wraps around the corner. Limiting a design to only two colors plus white adds to its simplicity and makes it easier to live with. Here, the dark green matches the sofa color so the earthy brown is the only new color introduced by the supergraphic. When you apply a light color over a dark one, put a coat of white primer between them.

This supergraphic balances a long and a short wall by reversing the colors. The heavier dark colors are used in the background of the short wall but are used as design colors on the long wall.

Paint and Color
Diagonal stripes

Supergraphics can also be executed with a number of bright colors, as demonstrated by the diagonal design shown opposite (top). The design is simple—a series of adjacent diagonal stripes with the end angles used in a variety of ways. The walls are stark white, as are the woodwork and furniture. The only other color note is the red upholstered chair. The room seemed to need strong colors. I worked out the design first; then I cut strips of construction paper in various colors and rearranged them until I was pleased with the effect of the colors working with each other. Since there was little color competition in the room, I was free to use any colors. In a room that has existing color, this same design could be executed in shades of only one or two colors and still be effective. But in using several colors, be sensitive to the way they work on each other. As a rule, a warm color between two cool colors will make the warm color look brighter, while several warm colors together tend to cancel the brightness of each other. But experiment first with strips of paper in the colors you want to use to see their effect on each other.

Paint and Color
Sunrise

The sunrise pictured on page 2323 combined geometric and free-form supergraphics, the sun and its rays being precisely drawn and the green hills loosely sketched. In this case the ceiling is used as an integral part of the design. Although the design rounds the corner with hills equally divided on two walls, the central design feature (the sun) is contained on one wall. The sun is made with two concentric circles; the rays are stripes that become wider as they extend farther from the sun. The green hills were drawn first with charcoal. The combination works because the shapes are stylized rather than realistic forms.

Paint and Color
Flowers

The basement playroom shown opposite (bottom) is decorated with large, stylized flowers painted in bright, warm colors. The walls are brick from the floor to about waist height, then plaster up to the ceiling; these two surfaces are separated by a narrow wood molding. The plaster walls were first painted with primer, then a base coat. The long, narrow panel to be decorated was then divided into two sections by painting a brown frame around each. Most of the floral design was concentrated on the panel that will be nearest an arrangement of a sofa and two chairs.

Working in Charcoal
You should work out any design on paper first before drawing it on the wall. But a free-form design like this one is more subject to change than a geometric design. To allow for modification, use charcoal to sketch the flowers on the wall. Charcoal can be wiped away more easily than pencil lines, letting you make quick alterations as the design progresses. Use charcoal to outline the flowing green background design, too. When you paint, work from the background out. Let any details, such as the centers of the flowers, wait until last.

Opposite, top: Many colors can be used together successfully, but work them out and test them with construction paper first. These five colors have full reign in a totally white room, the red chair being the only spot of competing color.

Opposite, bottom: Stylized flowers on a flowing green hillside brighten the top half of a wall in a basement playroom. This design was loosely sketched on the wall with charcoal, rather than being precisely drawn with pencil and ruler as were the geometric designs.

2331

Paint and Color
Free-form supergraphic

The free-form supergraphic shown below is used to define an area. The living room and dining room in this house occupy one long space; the graphic encloses the dining area and sets it apart. I used the freely flowing shapes in three shades of one quiet color because the room was already furnished with an eclectic collection of furniture, grouped around a patterned rug and decorated with a variety of plants, sculpture, and dried flower arrangements. The room already had so much pattern that a bold supergraphic would have confused the room rather than unified it. The three shades of brown were selected from the various shades and textures of brown used elsewhere in both the dining and living rooms.

Controlled Freedom
Although the design looks free form, it did not just happen. I sketched it carefully on paper first to make sure it would flow gracefully, then transferred it to the wall with charcoal that could easily be wiped away if I wanted to make a change. When you paint a design like this one, it is a good idea to have some of the background paint on hand. Then, if you paint beyond your line and do not like the way it looks, you can reduce the color with background paint.

Like ribbons fluttering in a breeze, rippling stripes in shades of brown define the dining area of a long room which also contains a living room. The quiet, low-key design does not conflict with the variety of patterns elsewhere in the room.

Paint and Color
Indian motif

The Navaho-inspired supergraphic shown below provides a focus for the treasures in the room—Indian artifacts collected by the owners, such as the ceramic covered bowl in the foreground of the photograph. The unusual color scheme of the graphic is based on a Navaho sand painting and a tie-dyed fabric wall hanging; it harmonizes well with the rich, earthy colors elsewhere in the room. With a supergraphic that not only is contained on one wall but is centered on it, it becomes very important to get the proportions correct. Follow the design in Figure A. To paint the design, always use masking tape between colors (sealing it in place to make sure the paint does not run, as described on page 2325). Paint from the inside to the outside of the design. Thus, the masking tape always goes on the background color rather than on a freshly painted design area.

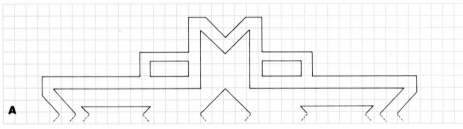

A

Figure A: Use this pattern if you would like to reproduce the Navaho-Indian-inspired design below as a supergraphic. Make an enlarged grid on the wall with a chalked plumb line (page 2324); then transfer the design to the wall, square by square.

This geometric design, adapted from a traditional American Indian motif, mirrors the flavor of a room filled with Indian artifacts and furnished in earthy colors.

Paint and Color
Fabric design

The idea for the supergraphic shown opposite came from a fabric—a vivid brown, beige, black, and white print—used to cover two sofa pillows and laminated to window shades. The design in the supergraphic is four times as large as the design in the fabric. To use such a design source, experiment to see how much you want to enlarge it for a supergraphic. You might take only a small section of fabric, for example, and enlarge it ten times or more.

Enlarging the Design

Enlarging a geometric design, with straight lines and precise circles and arcs, is relatively easy. You simply decide on the scale you want (1 inch equals 1 foot, for example), and position the dominant element of the design within the design area of the wall. All the remaining elements can be added easily with a yardstick and a little care.

To enlarge this free-form pattern, I took down a window shade, and put it on a piece of plywood on the floor. To make a grid without marking the shade (Figure B), I put horizontal and vertical strings across the shade and attached them to the plywood with thumbtacks. (If you have a scrap of leftover fabric, you can draw a grid directly on it with a pencil and ruler.) The grid over the fabric was made of 3-inch squares; the grid on the wall thus required 12-inch squares. I put the grid on the wall with a chalked plumb line (page 2324); (the chalk is easy to wipe off when the design is finished). With 12-inch squares marked on the wall, transfer the fabric design, square by square, using charcoal to draw the shapes. In this fabric, the design repeats every three vertical rows, so once I had this much of the pattern on the wall, I could simply copy it across the width of the wall.

For related crafts and projects, see the entries "Color Psychology," "Models and Mock-ups," and "Oil Painting."

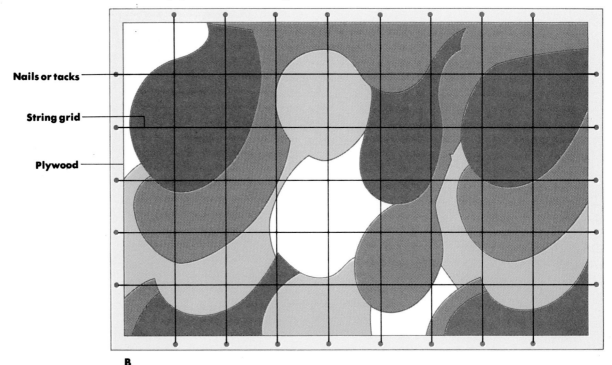

Nails or tacks

String grid

Plywood

B
Figure B: To make an enlargement grid on fabric that you do not want to mark, tack horizontal and vertical strings across the fabric at convenient intervals—here, 3 inches. Mark larger squares on the wall—in this case 12 inches to enlarge the pattern four times—and copy the design, square by square.

Opposite: This supergraphic is an enlargement of a fabric design used in the sofa pillows and laminated to two windows shades (not in the photograph). The graphic is four times as large as the fabric design.

SWEDISH HUCK WORK
Geometric Embroidery

Rosemary Drysdale was born and educated in England. She wrote her thesis on counted-thread embroidery at Durham University. Upon graduation, she taught embroidery to children. In 1963, Rosemary moved to the United States. She taught embroidery at the Nantucket Historical Trust and worked as a free-lance designer. She is the author of The Art of Blackwork Embroidery *and lives in New York.*

Swedish huck work is a form of counted-thread embroidery that is worked on a fabric that has intermittent visible threads, called floats, in a particular pattern in the weave. Unlike most embroidery, huck work incorporates these background threads into the design. This embroidery technique, always geometric, is also known as Swedish weaving, huck weaving, huck embroidery, or Swedish darning. Embroidery in one form or another has long been practiced in all of Europe, but the combination of geometric embroidery with a special background fabric was developed in Sweden.

The fabric on which huck weaving is done is called huckaback or huck toweling. Traditionally used for hand towels, in the past it was available only in white linen in widths up to 20 inches. Today huck toweling, available at mail-order needlework shops, comes in cotton as well as in linen, in many colors, and woven in widths up to 36 inches, so it can be used for many things other than hand towels. The fabric is

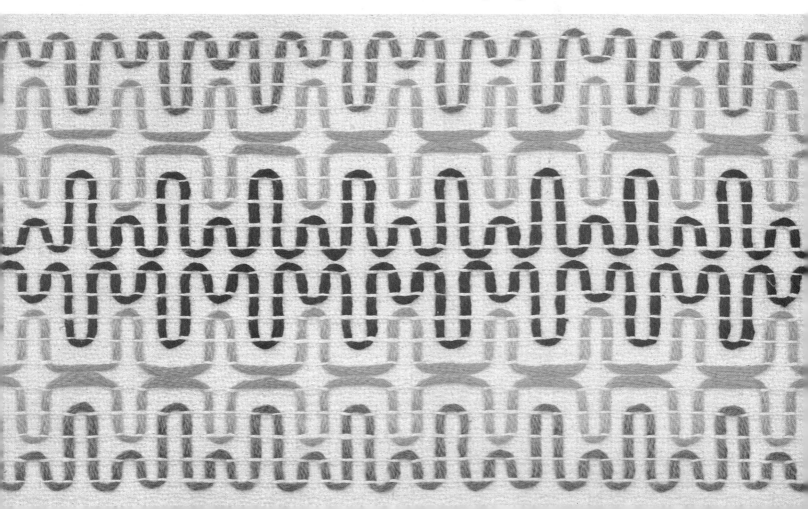

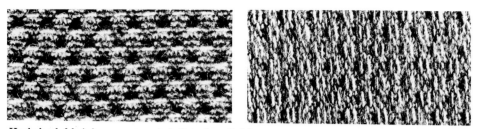

Huckaback fabric is woven so certain threads, called floats, stand out on the surface. Single floater threads run horizontally on one side (left); on the other side (right), double floater threads run vertically in pairs. In huck work, embroidery thread is anchored under these threads.

woven so certain threads, the floats, stand out on the surface. On one side, single-thread floats run across the fabric from one selvage (the woven edge) to the other. On the reverse side, double-thread floats run vertically in the fabric, parallel with the selvage edges. (These double-thread floats are treated as though they were single; they are always used together.) Either side of the fabric may be embroidered, and the fabric may be held so floater threads are either vertical or horizontal. You will find the side with the double threads allows a greater variety of embroidery patterns, however.

In huck work, the floats are guides; the embroidery thread is passed under them to make the design.

Only four stitches are used in huck work. These are illustrated in the Craftnotes (pages 2338 and 2339). Projects that follow, worked on both sides of the huckaback, include a hand towel (page 2340), a bag (page 2341), and a pillow (page 2343), plus suggestions for creating your own huck-work designs.

Swedish huck work is geometric embroidery worked horizontally in rows across a special fabric called huckaback. The embroidery thread is drawn under exposed threads on the huckaback surface; the latter becomes part of the design. This pattern decorates a hand towel; instructions are on page 2340.

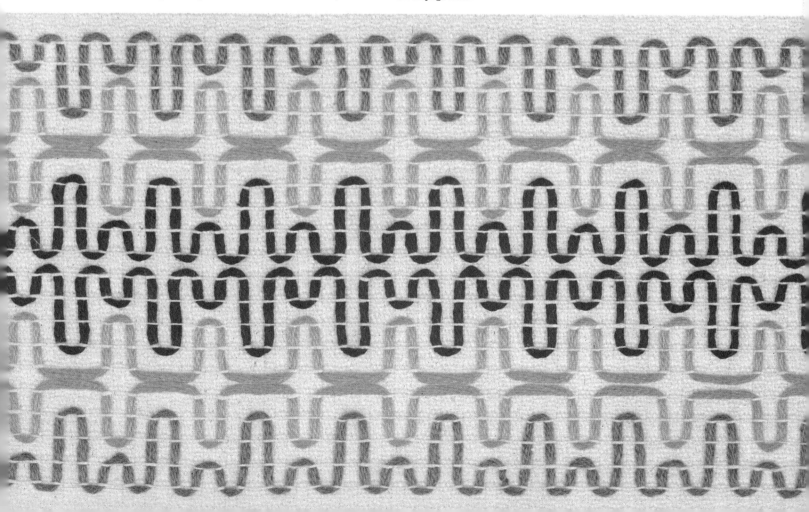

CRAFTNOTES: STITCHES

The embroidery stitches used in Swedish huck work are made in rows across the huckaback fabric. One row is completed before the next one is started. The pattern thus formed is always geometric; it is made with horizontal, vertical, diagonal, and long stitches.

The diagrams and photographs that follow show how these stitches are worked on the double-float side of the fabric. Since each pair of floats is treated as one, the stitches could be worked the same way on the single-float side of the fabric.

To make a horizontal stitch, take the needle under one set of float threads; then follow the floats that lie along the same horizontal line as the first pair.

Four rows of horizontal stitches are pictured at the right. Note that the position of the floats alternates with each row.

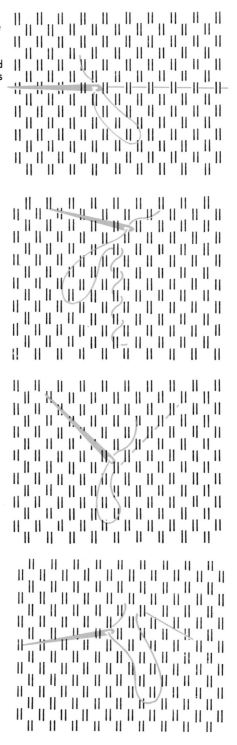
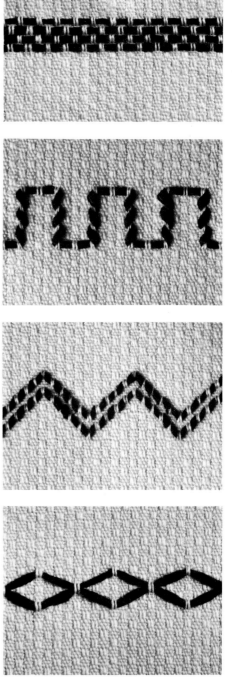

To make a vertical stitch, take the needle under one set of floats, working from right to left. Then take the thread up to the next set of floats directly above the one worked. Again, put the needle through from right to left.

Vertical stitches are usually combined with horizontal stitches as at right.

To make a diagonal stitch, put the needle under one set of floats, working from right to left. Then put it under a set of floats that is one row over and one row up (or down) from the first, so the thread forms a diagonal line.

Two rows of diagonal stitches, made zig-zag fashion, create the series of waves pictured.

To make a long stitch, put the needle from right to left under one set of floats. Skip one or more sets of floats, depending on the length of stitch you want, before picking up another set, horizontally, vertically, or diagonally.

Long diagonal stitches are used to make the diamond shapes pictured at right.

AND DESIGNS

Horizontal stitches are combined with short vertical ones to create this motif, worked on the double-float side of the fabric. The motif can be repeated many times.

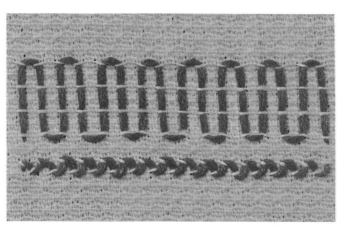

A very large and a very small row combine to make this unusual motif. It is worked on the single-float side of the fabric. You could work another small row on top of the large row.

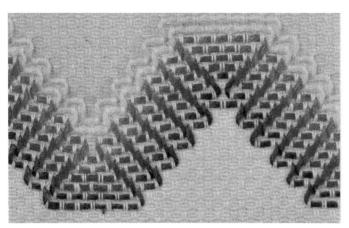

Worked on the double-float side of the fabric, this band of V's, made of steps of horizontal and vertical stitches, is given added impact by the rainbow of colors.

A combination of horizontal and long stitches, mostly diagonal, was worked in two colors to make this motif. It is worked on the side of the fabric with double floats.

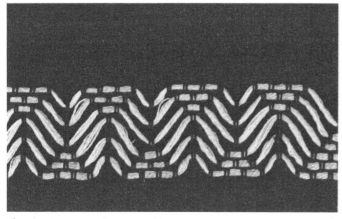

This design is a combination of horizontal stitches and long stitches worked diagonally on the double-float side of the fabric. You could create a new look by using different-colored thread.

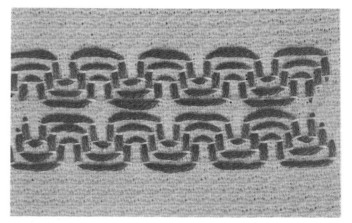

Worked on the single-float side of the fabric, this series of waves is made of long horizontal and vertical stitches. The bottom three waves are mirror-images of the top three.

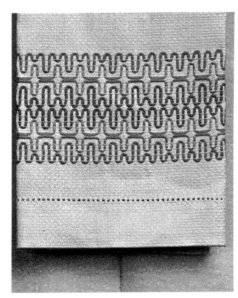

Red, yellow, and orange huck embroidery was worked on the side of a linen hand towel that had single floater threads running horizontally. The design required only eight rows of embroidery.

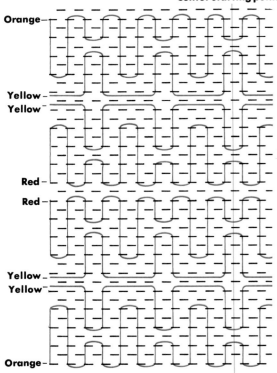

Center starting point

Orange —
Yellow —
Yellow —
Red —
Red —
Yellow —
Yellow —
Orange —

A

Figure A: This pattern was used to embroider the hand towel shown above. Short horizontal lines indicate the floats—threads of the base fabric under which embroidery thread passes. Colored lines indicate the embroidery thread. To embroider this pattern, start at the center and work out to the left, repeating the motif as many times as you like. Then turn the fabric bottom edge up and work from the center out to the left again to finish the row. (If you are left-handed, reverse this procedure.)

Needlecrafts
Hand towel

Huck embroidery was traditionally worked on small hand towels made of linen. The 14-by-22-inch towel shown at left was purchased ready-made. The hem, with its decorative hemstitched edge, was made so the side of the fabric with single-thread floats is on the outside. That dictated that the embroidery be done on that side. In addition to the towel, you will need 6-strand embroidery thread in three colors—orange, yellow, and red were used here—and a No. 22 (or finer) tapestry needle. (The finer the needle you use, the more easily it will go under the floater threads.) The strip of embroidery is 2½ inches deep.

Estimating Thread Needs
Since all the embroidery is worked on the front of the fabric, use a thread that is long enough to complete one row. There is no precise way to determine this length in advance, since each pattern requires a different amount of thread. Start with a thread about 2½ times as long as the line to be embroidered. Measure the amount left over when you finish the row. Subtract the length left over from the length you started with and you will have the approximate length of thread needed to embroider a matching row.

Working a Row of Embroidery
To establish the first row of the embroidery, start at the center of the fabric and work out to one edge, then the other. Thread the needle with embroidery thread and pull it under the float in the center of the design. Draw half the thread through from right to left; leave the other half loose at the right. Work the design from right to left, following Figure A. When you get to the end of the design on the left side, you will need to finish the thread neatly because there is no hem or side seam to catch it in. To do this, loop the thread around the last float used and then take it back through the last three or four floats of the design (Figure B). This gives you a

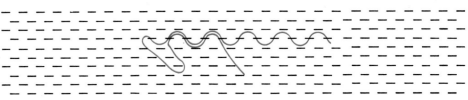

B

Figure B: To end the embroidery thread neatly on the right side, loop the thread around the last float, then take it back under three or four floats. Clip the end of the thread near the last float it passed under.

double thickness of embroidery thread at the end, but it eliminates the need to knot the thread on the back, so the design looks equally smooth on back and front. To complete the row of embroidery, turn the fabric bottom edge up, and thread the other half of the embroidery thread through the needle. Follow the design in Figure A, again working from right to left. (If you are left-handed, you may find it more convenient to reverse this procedure, working from left to right on both halves of the design.) When you have finished the second half of the first row, end the thread as before.

After you have established the first row of the design, you do not necessarily have to start each row in the middle. You could work entire rows from right to left. However, when you work a row in halves, you use only half the thread at a time, minimizing the possibility of tangling or accidentally knotting the thread. The design shown has eight rows of embroidery thread, in three colors. You could do fewer rows or more, as you like.

Caring for Embroidered Towels
To care for such towels and other embroidered work, wash them by hand. You can use hot water, since the fabric will be either cotton or linen. Press on the wrong side while the fabric is still damp.

Needlecrafts
A handbag

$ 🖎 🚶 🫖

With handles and a small amount of needlework, you can turn huckaback fabric into a handbag. Handles of the type pictured below can be purchased at needlework stores. The finished bag shown measures 13 by 14 inches. You cut the fabric to size, work the embroidery on it; then sew the pieces together and attach the handles.

To make the bag, you will need: 1 yard of 17-inch-wide huckaback (or ½ yard of a 36-inch width); 6-strand embroidery cotton or No. 5 pearl cotton in three colors; a No. 22 tapestry needle; ½ yard of cotton fabric for the lining; thread; and wooden handles. Cut the huckaback fabric into two pieces 15 inches wide by 14 inches long, including ½-inch seam allowances. Start the design 2½ inches up from one 15-inch edge; it will be 2 inches from the bottom of the bag after the ½-inch seam is sewn. Work the embroidery from the center of the bag out to the two sides, as described on page 2340. Follow the design given in Figure C, page 2342. You do not need to secure the ends of embroidery thread by doubling them back; they will be caught in the side seams. If you like, you can embroider the back piece the same way.

Place the two pieces of huckaback together, right sides facing, and stitch along the bottom and up both sides for 10 inches, making a ½-inch seam. Turn the bag right side out. Fold and press the unsewn side edges ½ inch to the inside, to match the seam, but do not sew. For the lining, cut two pieces of cotton fabric 15 inches wide by 13 inches long. With right sides facing, stitch the lining along the bottom and up the sides for 10 inches, again making a ½-inch seam. Fold and press the raw edges under ½ inch along the remainder of the sides and along the top. Slip the lining inside the bag so the wrong sides of bag and lining are facing; when you open the bag, you will see the right side of the lining. Put one of the top edges of the bag through the slot in the handle from the outside. Fold that edge over the wooden rung so you can stitch the fabric to itself inside the pocketbook. The edge will be gathered slightly because the slot in the handle is 10½ inches long and the fabric going through it is 13 inches wide. Stitch the raw edge just below the wooden rung. Do not sew the lining in at this point. Repeat this procedure to attach the other handle. Then stitch the lining to the bag, working along the pressed edges of the top and sides of the lining, and positioning it to conceal the edges of the outer fabric. For the top of the lining to fit the top of the bag (now 10½ inches), you will need to take a tuck in the lining fabric, as shown in the photograph below (right).

Below, left: Wooden handles provide the finishing touch for a simple but capacious bag made of huckaback fabric elegantly decorated with embroidery thread. You could choose colors that will match your favorite outfit, or let them be neutral so you can use the bag with everything.

Below, right: The light blue of the embroidery thread at the center of the design band is repeated in the blue lining, which has a tuck in its center so it fits the gathered top of the huckaback fabric.

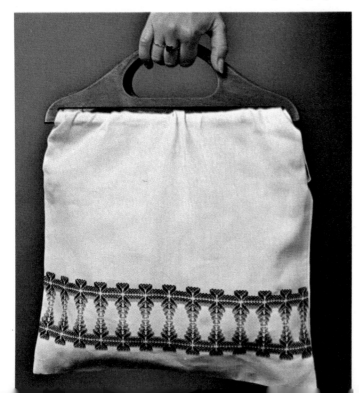

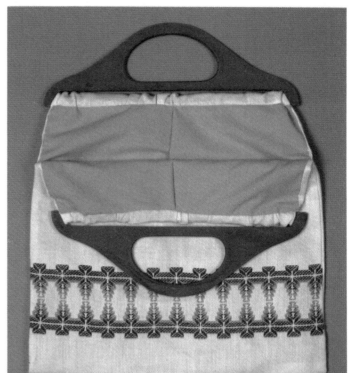

Center starting point

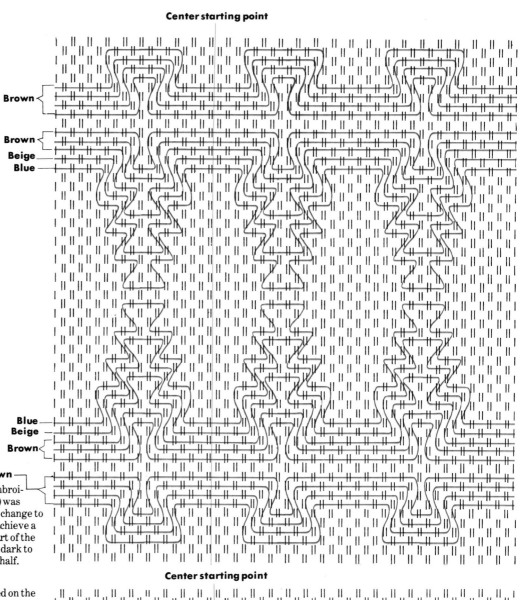

Brown

Brown
Beige
Blue

Blue
Beige
Brown

Brown

Figure C: Following this pattern, the embroidered design on the handbag (page 2341) was worked almost entirely in brown, with a change to beige and blue only near the center. To achieve a different look, you could work the top part of the band in a rainbow of colors ranging from dark to light, reversing the colors in the bottom half.

Figure D: This pattern for the design used on the pillow pictured opposite shows how the interlocking effect was achieved by working the last row of the first motif and the first row of the next motif under the same floater threads.

Center starting point

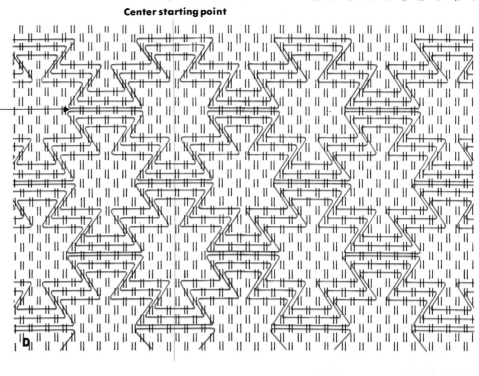

Last thread of one row and first thread of next row sharing space

Needlecrafts
The pillow

$ ⧖ ♀ 🔔

Although traditionally used to make borders, Swedish huck work can be extended to make larger designs, as illustrated by the pillow shown below. Like all huck work, the pillow is embroidered in rows, but each row is connected to the row above it to form a single overall design. The pillow is 13 inches square; the design area, 11 inches square. To make the pillow, you will need: ½ yard of huckaback; 6-strand embroidery cotton or No. 5 pearl cotton; ½ yard of pillow-backing fabric; thread; and a 13-inch-square pillow form or loose polyester filling.

Cut a 14-inch-square of huckaback for the 13-inch-square pillow (the extra inch allows a ½-inch seam all around). Start the first row 2½ inches down from the top edge and midway between the side edges; this row will be 2 inches from the edge of the pillow when the seam is closed. Follow the design in Figure D, working from the center to the left, stopping 2 inches from the fabric edge. Then turn the fabric bottom edge up, and work the other half from right to left. Next, note that the last thread of the top motif and the first thread of the next motif share the same floater threads; this unifies the design at the edge with each subsequent row.

If you underestimate the amount of thread needed for a row, you can start a new thread as follows. End the old thread in an inconspicuous place, such as a horizontal line, and start the new thread in the same place (Figure E), letting the ends share three or four floats. Trim the loose ends close to the floats. At the end of each row, end the thread by doubling back for several floats, as shown in Figure B, page 2340.

To finish the pillow, cut a piece of backing fabric 14 inches square. Place the embroidered fabric and the backing fabric together, right sides facing, and stitch them together ½ inch from the edge, leaving an 8-inch opening (Figure F). Trim the corners and turn the pillow cover right side out. Insert the pillow form or pack the pillow with loose polyester stuffing; then stitch the opening closed by hand.

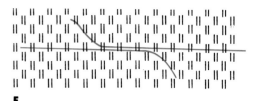

E

Figure E: If you must start a new thread partway across a row, run it under the last three or four floats occupied by the old thread. Then clip the ends of both threads near the floats.

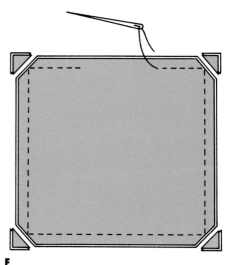

F

Figure F: With right sides facing, stitch the embroidered pillow front and the backing fabric together by sewing along all sides, leaving an 8-inch opening for stuffing. Trim the corners as shown before you turn the cover right side out. Stuff, then stitch closed.

In making this pillow cover, navy blue embroidery thread was worked in rows across the white fabric. The huck-work motifs are interlocked, so you are not aware where one row ends and the next begins.

SWINGS
Swoops and Glides

Paul Hogan has been building playgrounds for much of his life. When he was a child, his yard was a neighborhood play center. When he became a father, he built such a playground. Now he has formed a nonprofit corporation, Playground Clearing House, Inc., in Phoenixville, Pennsylvania, and has helped more than 250 communities build playgrounds. The author of Playgrounds for Free, published by the Massachusetts Institute of Technology, Paul Hogan has collected a treasure trove of books, slides, films, and ideas about play equipment.

"How do you like to go up in a swing
Up in the air so blue?
Oh, I do think it the pleasantest thing
Ever a child can do!"

Most children seem to agree with Robert Louis Stevenson, for swings are the single most popular piece of playground equipment. I know more than a few adults, too, who can't resist taking a swing when they can. What other easily available means is there of achieving such an exhilarating sensation of freedom and flight? Swings have been around for a long time. In primitive form, they must have been commonplace in early man's jungle playground. Long before more sophisticated means of transportation were found, the original Tarzans flew through the air, swinging from one vine to another.

What Is a Swing?
Webster's dictionary has more than two dozen definitions for swing. My own definition of a play swing is anything you can either grab onto with your hands or sit or stand on as you move through the air. I have seen hundreds of variations, but the best swing is the one you build yourself with whatever materials are most handy.

Because of their great popularity, playground swings are often expensive and hard to maintain. But the swings on these pages are sturdy and inexpensive. Unlike more conventional swings, they are intended to promote social interaction and help develop muscle coordination, important by-products of play.

A swing can be anything from a heavy rope looped over a tree (page 2346) to a huge tire supported by a chain (page 2347). For those who would like to introduce swinging to very young children, there is an indoor swing made of wrapped and knotted rope and yarn (page 2355).

On Safety
The most important consideration in building a swing is safety, and that begins with installation over a soft surface. If that surface already is dirt or sand, fine. But swings should never be hung over blacktop or concrete. Even softer than dirt or sand are several inches of tanbark, pine needles, sawdust, or foam rubber scraps. I have recently been using surplus rubber conveyor belting under swings.

The next most important thing is to make sure that the swing supports and components are strong enough to take the wear expected. A permanent swing must be able to withstand much more wear than a temporary one, such as a rope looped over a tree limb meant to be used for only a day or two. If you improvise your own construction, make sure the design is sound. All of the swings shown on these pages have withstood the test of time and hard use.

Wherever possible, we add safety chains (page 2347). In the event that a hook wears out or a nut works loose, the safety chain permits the swing seat to drop just a few inches. At public playgrounds, youngsters can even wear out universal joints salvaged from army tanks; the safety chain prevents any accident when that happens.

Three final suggestions to help you build a safe swing: Make the seat of a resilient material like rubber, not wood and certainly not steel. Keep the seat close to the ground. Position the swing so it is far enough away from obstacles, including the support structure, so no one will get bumped while swinging.

Rubber hose

Eye splice

A
Figure A: To make a rope swing, draw a heavy rope over a tree limb 3 to 4 inches in diameter. Choose a location just beyond a heavy outside crotch to keep the loop from slipping down toward the trunk. Slip a length of rubber hose over the end of rope to protect it from wear as it crosses the limb. Make an eye splice in one end of the rope (page 2346); slip the other end through it.

The next time you discard a worn-out tire, tie a length of rope to it to make a swing that is far superior to the conventional kind. It is inexpensive, swings in any direction, is relatively safe, and holds two or more children. As Amy and Roger would agree, a tire swing is loads of fun. Directions for making two kinds of tire swings begin on page 2346.

Making an eye splice

To form an eye splice, you bend an end of rope back and splice it into the rope, so the end of the rope becomes a loop. Prepare to make the eye splice by unraveling about 8 inches of the strands at the end of the rope; then double the rope back on itself. To weave the splice, hold the rope just below the splice area and twist the main part (called the standing part) clockwise. This will open the main part enough so you can tuck in one strand from the end of the rope (**a** below). Use a stick, or a marlinspike if you own one, to keep the strands separated during the tuck, withdrawing it when the end strand is in place.

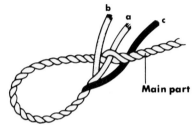

Tuck the first strand (**a**) uphill and against the spiral of the rope, called its lay, as illustrated. Position the second and third strands (**b**) and (**c**) over and under the main part of the rope, as shown above.

Lift the second strand (**b**) and tuck it into the lay of the rope, twisting to open the strands and going uphill against the lay of the main rope as before. Note that the second strand (**b**) is inserted closer to the loop than the first strand (**a**) and in a different part of the main rope. At this stage the third strand (**c**) is underneath the main part.

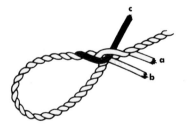

Turn the loop over so that the third strand (**c**) now lies on top of the main part, and tuck it in, doubling it under, as shown, so you again go uphill against the lay of the main part. When this tuck is complete, turn the loop over and begin a second three-step sequence with the first strand (**a**). Continue until all the loose strands of rope are woven into the main part. Trim any short ends close to the rope.

A swing doesn't have to be a permanent installation. A simple rope swing such as this one at the Paoli Elementary School in Pennsylvania can be quickly made ready for play at a picnic site.

Outdoor Activities
Rope swing

All you need to make a rope swing is a sturdy tree, a heavy rope, a length of rubber hose, a ladder (or a rock and some heavy cord), and someone with a desire to play Tarzan.

Prepare one end of the rope by making an eye splice (shown at left). Then draw the rope over a 3- to 4-inch limb of a healthy tree (Figure A, page 2344). A good safety rule of thumb is to place the rope one foot away from the trunk for every two feet of rope used, to help forestall bumps. Note, in Figure A, that a second branch keeps the rope from sliding back toward the trunk. If the branch is high and no ladder is available, you can resort to a mariner's heaving-line technique. Tie a ½-pound rock to some heavy cord. Warn everyone out of the way, then heave the weighted cord over the branch. Tie the free end of the cord to the loop end of the swing rope. Haul the swing rope over the branch and down where you can reach it.

Slip the free end of the rope through the loop and pull until the loop is snug against the branch. Then cut the rope to the desired length. Make sure the rope is exactly where you want it; once the loop is snug, you won't be able to move it without climbing up to it.

Such a rope swing is perfectly usable and is a good way to develop arm muscles. A knot or two for hand holds may prevent rope burns. Or you can make a foot loop at the free end of the rope to support most of the body weight, as pictured above. Form a large eye splice as you did at the other end, but make sure the loop is large enough so the swinger can get a foot in (and out) easily.

Outdoor Activities
Tire swings

The conventional swing is designed for only one activity—a solitary child sitting down and swinging back and forth in an arc. If the swinger tries to move sideways,

This horizontal tire swing is suspended from a cantilevered pole, but for home use it could be hung from a tree. It provides all the swing and swirl these girls could want. This super swing was built for the Hillside School in Berwyn, Pennsylvania. It allows three or four children at one time to swing safely in every direction.

Jim rides on top of a vertical tire swing that is suspended from a chain bolted into a strong tree limb. This variation of the tire swing shown on page 2345 was built by Paul Hogan for the Charlestown playground in Phoenixville, Pennsylvania.

or if two children attempt to ride the same swing, with at least one of them standing up, the possibility of an accident multiplies.

A tire swing, on the other hand, is intended to go in all directions. One type, the horizontal tire swing, provides room for several children to swing together. Tire swings have a smaller range of motion than conventional swings, so there is less danger of a collision.

Vertical Tire Swing

The traditional tire swing pictured on page 2345 is an embellishment of the rope swing (opposite). Once the rope is secured to the tree limb, slip the lower end through the tire and fasten it with an eye splice (opposite).

If none of your trees has a sturdy branch extending out far enough to give clearance for a tire swing so it will not bump the trunk, you can stretch a heavy rope between two trees and sling the tire in the middle.

Horizontal Tire Swing

The tire swing that is slung so the tire stays horizontal is very popular and has many variations. Children ride it by sitting on the tire and clinging to the supporting ropes or chains. The horizontal tire swing shown above left, was built in a public schoolyard; the tire hangs from a cantilevered telephone pole, strong enough to hold several childen at one time. For home use, such a swing could more easily be suspended from a strong limb on a large tree.

As shown in Figure B, a universal joint is used to permit a smoother back and forth motion of the tire; lower down, a swivel prevents the chains from twisting around each other as the tire spins. Other tools and materials needed are: a ⅝-inch threaded rod or bolt long enough to penetrate the tree limb and project 3 or 4 inches; a ⅜-inch steel ring 2 inches in diameter; two ⅝-inch washers; a ⅝-inch nut; three clevis bolts (see Craftnotes, page 2353); about 15 feet of ⅜-inch chain (the actual length depends on the height of the tree limb); three 6-foot lengths of 3/16-inch chain; three chain repair links; a car or truck tire; three ¼-inch eyebolts; six ¼-inch nuts; and twelve ¼-inch washers. You will also need a hand or electric drill

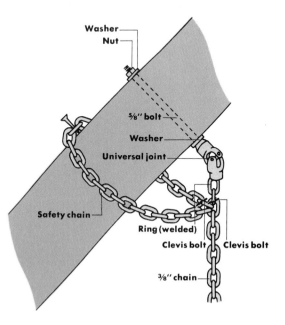

B

Figure B: To support a horizontal tire swing that several children will use at once, put a ⅝-inch bolt, welded to a universal joint, through a tree limb. Connect a heavy chain to a welded-on ring, using a clevis bolt. Then take the extra chain around the limb and connect it to itself with another clevis bolt, as an extra measure of safety.

2347

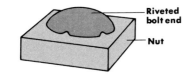

C

Figure C: To make sure a nut will not work loose from a bolt, you can use a ball peen hammer to flatten the end of the bolt.

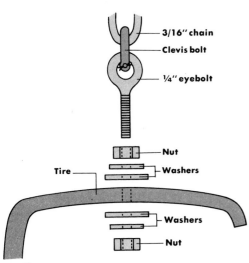

D

Figure D: Use a clevis bolt (Craftnotes, page 2353) and a welded eyebolt to attach a chain to a tire, as in the horizontal swing.

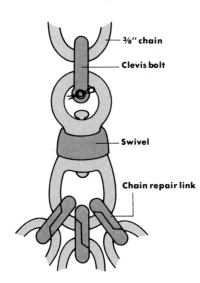

E

Figure E: A swivel and clevis bolt (top), and three chain-repair links (bottom) join the three lighter chains (attached to a tire) to a heavy chain, leaving the tire free to revolve.

with ⅝- and ¼-inch drill bits and a ball peen hammer. To protect the tree from infection after drilling a hole in the branch, use a pruning spray.

To make the swing, attach the ⅜-inch chain to a tree limb (Figure B, page 2347). First have the long bolt welded to the top of the universal joint, and the 2-inch ring welded to the bottom. Drill a hole for the bolt through the tree limb, at least 10 feet from the trunk. Spray the hole with pruning solution. Using a nut and washers as shown, attach the bolt to the tree limb. (It does the tree no harm when you drill a hole straight through a limb, as long as you remember to loosen the nut periodically as the limb grows; abrasion from anything circling a branch, however, could girdle the branch and kill it.) About 3 feet from the top link, use a clevis bolt to connect the ⅜-inch chain to the ring end of the universal joint.

To form a safety chain, take the top 3 feet of chain around the tree limb and connect the chain to itself, snug around the limb, using a second clevis bolt. After tightening the nut, make sure it will not work loose by flattening the end with a ball peen hammer (Figure C).

Drill three holes in the side of the tire with a ¼-inch bit, spacing them at equal intervals around the tire. Attach the three lengths of 3/16-inch chain to the tire using nuts and eyebolts, as shown in Figure D.

Using chain repair links, connect the free ends of the three chains to the swivel. Then connect the single chain above to the swivel, using the third clevis bolt (Figure E). Make sure the tire is suspended 2 feet off the ground, and that the three chains are of equal length so the tire hangs level. If the swing is too low, the children's weight will cause it to sag uncomfortably close to the ground. If it is too high, smaller children will have difficulty climbing on, and the swing will be dangerous. If necessary, adjust the height.

The completed swing should never bump against the tree trunk. If there is some danger that it might, the swinging action can be reduced with a restraining chain. You attach one end of such a chain to the bottom of the tire and the other to a swivel in a concrete plug set in the ground.

Outdoor Activities
Pulley-and-cable glides $ ⌧ 🚶 ⚒

There are two basic ways to rig a pulley-and-cable swinging glide. Rope cable wears out and breaks fairly quickly; steel cable is advisable. The rider swings in the air as he slides down the inclined cable strung between two trees or posts. The cable supplies the track and a pulley provides the glide. The pulley should be removable so it can be easily replaced when it wears out. You will need to oil or grease the pulley whenever it starts to slow down. A ball-bearing pulley is preferable, but sometimes it is hard to find.

On steep steel-cable glides, I sometimes eliminate the pulley and substitute a ⅝-inch clevis bolt (Craftnotes, page 2353). These are inexpensive and easily replaced, and if the incline is steep, they slide along as fast as you would care to go.

Steel Cable Rig
If you use a steel cable, it should be at least ⅜-inch high-tensile steel, made of twisted wires, and the two eyebolts that connect the cable to the anchor points should be at least ⅝ inch in diameter. Drill the holes for the eyebolts with a bit of the same diameter. If the anchor points are trees, buy eyebolts whose lengths are equal to the diameter of the tree trunks, plus 3 or 4 inches so you can loosen the nut periodically as the tree increases in girth. Spray any hole you drill in a tree with pruning solution, and the tree will not be harmed. But never encircle a tree trunk with a cable; this could cut through the outer layer of bark and kill the tree. You will also need: a two-eyed ½-inch turnbuckle; one ⅜-inch clevis bolt or chain repair link; five ⅜-inch cable clamps; two washers; one very large washer (for a safety stop); heavy manila rope; and nuts to fit the long eyebolts (Craftnotes, page 2353).

The steel cable assembly is diagrammed in Figure F. Drill the holes for the eyebolts at least 8 feet off the ground. Insert the eyebolts and put washers and nuts on the ends to keep them in place. At the top anchor, join the eyebolt to one of the eyes

A hand grip made of strap steel and copper pipe often inspires freewheeling acrobatics on this cable-and-pulley glide.

Simple playthings often lead to childhood flights of fantasy. Here, Sandra indulges in some fancy footwork on a steel cable-and-pulley glide installed at the Hillside School in Pennsylvania.

of the turnbuckle, using a clevis bolt or chain repair link. Then connect the cable to the other end of the turnbuckle with at least two cable clamps (Figure G). The turnbuckle is used to adjust the tautness of the cable, thus controlling the speed of the rider.

Using an eye splice (page 2346), connect a long, heavy rope to the pulley so that a child of any age can hang at his own height. Having a long rope also makes it easier

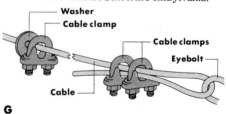

G

Figure G: To attach a steel cable to an eyebolt, pass it through two cable clamps, then the eye, and back through the clamps. Tighten the nuts on the saddles of the cable clamps, squeezing the cable until the fastening is secure.

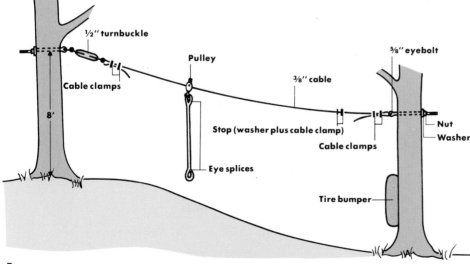

F

Figure F: To make a glide with a steel cable and pulley, use ⅝-inch eyebolts to fasten the cable to trees or posts. Cable clamps hold the cable in place. A turnbuckle permits adjustment of the cable tension, so the rider's speed can be controlled. The pulley stop on the cable and the bumper made of an old tire are safety devices.

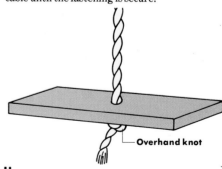

H

Figure H: To make a seat for a cable-and-pulley glide, drill a hole in a short wooden board. Pass the heavy rope that is connected to the pulley through the hole and tie an overhand knot underneath. The weight of the rider will force the board onto the knot and tighten it.

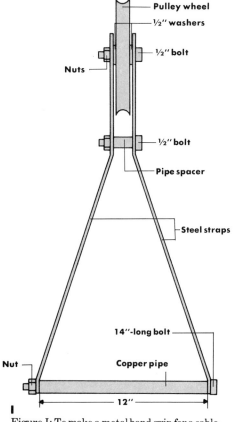

When he's not building swings, Paul Hogan can often be found riding them. Here he is gliding along on a 200-foot-long cable-and-pulley ride he and his children installed in their own backyard.

Figure I: To make a metal hand grip for a cable-and-pulley glide, bolt galvanized steel straps onto a pulley wheel. Then splay the ends of the steel straps and bolt a length of pipe in between.

to run back to the top of the incline with the pulley in tow. At this point, place the pulley on the cable.

Next, at least 4 feet from the bottom anchor, attach a stop to the cable, making it with a large washer held in place by a cable clamp (Figure G, page 2349). This washer will stop the pulley in time to keep the rider from crashing into the bottom tree. As a further safety precaution, tie a tire bumper onto the lower anchor. (If that lower anchor happens to be a post, you can put a dozen old tires over it before you connect the free end of the cable to it.)

Connect the free end of the cable to the second eyebolt anchor with two cable clamps as before. A second turnbuckle is not needed. If you like, the bottom end of the rope can be finished with a big eye-splice foot loop, as pictured on page 2349. For a deluxe model, a wooden plank can be attached for a seat (Figure H, page 2349).

Yet another variation is the metal handgrip pictured on page 2349 and diagramed in Figure I. To make it you need two flat pieces of galvanized strap steel, each measuring ¼ by 1½ by 24 inches (available at hardware stores). In each piece, drill a ½-inch hole 1 inch from the top. To do this, use an electric drill with increasingly larger metal-cutting bits; begin with a ⅛-inch bit, then use a ¼-inch bit, and so on. Thread a 2½-inch-long ½-inch-diameter bolt through the holes, with the pulley and ½-inch washers sandwiched between the straps. This bolt replaces the pulley's axle. Secure the bolt with a nut.

Drill another hole in each piece of steel, 2 or 3 inches below the pulley rim. Again, thread a 2½-inch-long bolt through the holes, but this time, place a pipe spacer with a ⅝-inch inside diameter between the straps, ¼ inch longer than the width of the pulley and washers.

Bend the ends of the steel straps out to 12 inches. Drill a hole in each end 1 inch from the bottom. Place a 12-inch-long copper pipe with a ⅝-inch inside diameter between the splayed ends. Put a ½-inch bolt 14 inches long through the pipe and secure it with a nut as shown in Figure I. Tie a piece of rope to the pipe so the pulley can be towed back to the top of the incline.

Rigging a Rope Cable

The rope-and-pulley glide, diagramed in Figure J, is simpler to put up and a bit slower, but it is also a lot of fun. To make it you will need enough heavy rope to span the distance between the two anchor points plus 15 feet, so several people can help pull it tight; a large pulley; and a second length of heavy rope to attach to the pulley. If the anchors are poles rather than trees, you will need to insert eyebolts as before to hold the rope.

To begin, attach the shorter length of rope to the pulley, using an eye splice (page 2346). At the top anchor tree, loop the cable rope around the trunk above a 10-foot-high limb. Tie it securely with a single bowline knot (Figure K). If you are using a pole as an anchor, feed the rope through the eyebolt and secure it with a bowline knot.

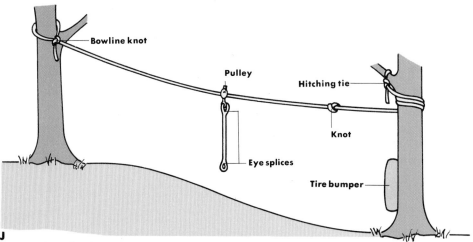

Figure J: To make a backyard rope-and-pulley glide for temporary use, tie a heavy rope between two trees. The pulley with another length of rope attached will roll down this incline. Note the use of branches to keep the rope from sliding down the tree trunk.

Slip the pulley on the cable rope. Tie a large knot in it. Pull the cable around the other tree until it is taut; then wrap it around the tree several times. Bring the rope end back toward the stretched cable and tie it to a branch, using a hitching tie (Figure L). The hitching tie is used because rain will affect the tautness of the rope. A tug on the short end of the rope will untie the hitch so you can adjust the tautness.

Outdoor Activities
Monkey swing $ ● 👫 ✈

When I was a child, I always had a monkey swing in my backyard. My children have one too, and enjoy it as much as I did. Swinging by one arm and reaching out to grab the next dangling ring or rope is an exhilarating experience. The Armed Forces use their version of the monkey swing to develop muscle and visual coordination.

The most important parts of a monkey swing are the anchor poles. Trees work best, but if you have no trees large enough, you can use strong posts set well in the ground. The lateral stress of children bouncing along the rings is tremendous. If the posts are not well anchored, they will loosen and lean toward each other, letting the cable between them sag. For the monkey swings I build, I usually use sections of utility poles. If only two anchor poles are used (one at each end), we try to obtain the services of a utility company auger truck to set them at least 6 feet deep with at least 8 feet projecting above the ground.

You also need a way to reach the first ring. We have used tires bolted to the pole, as pictured below, or empty oil drums—which are fun to bang on.

But if you do not have access to an auger, use a pick and shovel to dig a 4-foot-deep trench long enough to accommodate four posts in a row at each end (Figure M, page 2352). Set in the anchor posts, and then the shorter posts to backstop the anchor posts. These backstop poles serve another function—they form a staircase to the first ring.

Paul Hogan's daughter Lisa climbs the anchor post of a monkey-swing assembly made of heavy manila rope and steel rings.

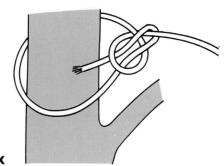

K
Figure K: When you use a rope cable, tie the top end of the rope to a tree using a single bowline knot, which is very strong.

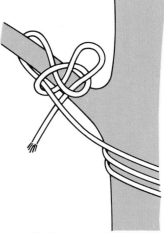

L
Figure L: Tie the lower end of the rope cable to the second tree using a hitching tie, a kind of slip knot that holds well but lets you untie it when you need to adjust the tension of the rope.

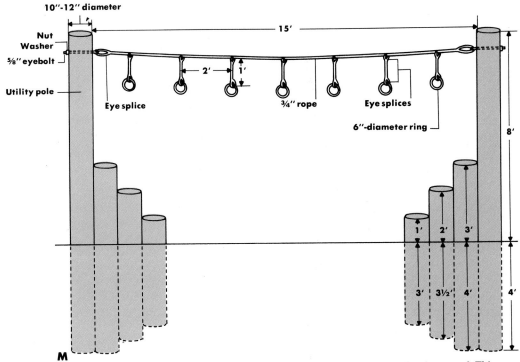

Figure M: If you make a monkey swing, make sure the anchor poles are set well in the ground. This type of swing may have many children bouncing on it at one time, so the anchor poles need to be firmly braced. Here, backstop poles double as steps.

To make the swing, you will need: about 20 feet of ¾-inch manila or nylon rope; two ⅝-inch eyebolts (the length depending on the diameter of the anchor poles); two ⅝-inch washers; two ⅝-inch nuts; seven 2-foot lengths of ½-inch manila or nylon rope; seven 6-inch rings (sold by farm implement suppliers as tow-chain rings); and a drill with a ⅝-inch bit.

Placing the first rope at the center, attach the seven 2-foot lengths of rope at 2-foot intervals to the heavy rope. To do this, use an eye splice (page 2346); open up the heavy rope where the length will be attached, slip the rope through the opening, and then form the eye splice. If this is done, the ropes will not slip sideways during use. Attach a ring to each length of rope, again using an eye splice. If you wish, wrap the ends of the rope with electrician's tape to keep them from raveling.

Following Figure M, drill a hole through one anchor post about 6 inches from the top. Insert the eyebolt; secure it with washer and nut. Join one end of the rope with the monkey rings attached to the eyebolt with an eye splice. Connect the free end of the rope to the other pole in the same way.

This drawing of another type of monkey swing was adapted from a Russian book on playground construction.

CRAFTNOTES: MATERIALS AND HARDWARE FOR OUTDOOR SWINGS

Do not compromise on quality. Most of the supplies you need can be bought at hardware stores and marine supply shops.

Rope: I prefer nylon rope over manila rope because it is stronger and rot proof. But it is more expensive and not always available. To cut the heavy rope used in swings, use a sharp heavy knife, a hatchet, or a hacksaw. You can keep a nylon rope from fraying by fusing ends with a pocket lighter or match flame. Heat just enough so the rope smolders and bubbles—don't set it on fire. The nylon may melt to the point where it will drip, so protect your hands with gloves. To prevent the ends of a manila rope from fraying, wrap the point you wish to cut with several layers of electrician's tape, applied in a spiral. Then cut or saw through the rope, tape and all, leaving the tape on the rope ends.

Clevis bolts: One of the most important pieces of equipment is the clevis bolt, used to join chains, pulleys, eyebolts, and other pieces of hardware. They are much safer than S-hooks, which all too often come apart. The two U-shaped clevis bolts pictured (above, left) have threaded screw pins. An even more secure type is held together with a cotter pin, which can't work loose the way a threaded pin can. In addition to linking parts, a large clevis bolt can be used instead of a pulley for sliding down a cable glide.

Pulleys: The snatch-block pulley (shown in its opened position above, center) is designed so it can be replaced when it wears out, without disassembling the cable it rides on. Secure this type of pulley by wrapping the opening device with heavy wire so it can't be opened without the use of wire cutters. A second type is the more conventional closed-block pulley (above, right); the cable must be threaded through it. A third type (pictured on page 2349) can be made from a large grooved wheel with ball bearings; it provides the smoothest ride of all.

Eyebolts: In large sizes, eyebolts are used to connect a chain, steel cable, or rope to tires, poles, and trees. Above (the bottom four) are eyebolts ranging in size from ¼ inch (used on a tire) to ⅝ inch (used on cable glides and monkey swings).

Eyes that have been welded closed are far safer than mechanically closed eyes, which tend to open under stress. Eyebolts bear the most weight in a swing assembly, and even the heaviest must be watched and replaced when it starts to wear (the second from top, above, is worn through). Utility companies use strong D-rings (above, top). If you can buy them, these ⅝-inch D-shaped eyes can be used in place of eyebolts.

Turnbuckles: These devices let you adjust the tension of a cable without disconnecting it from its anchor points. A turnbuckle used in a cable glide should have welded eyes (above, bottom) and be at least ½ inch in diameter and 12 inches long. To prevent accidental separation, smash the ends of the threads with a hammer and cold chisel.

Steel cable: The best type to use is 5,000-pound-test galvanized steel cable. Use the flexible type, made of many steel wires twisted together. You can sometimes buy steel cable from utility companies and at automobile supply houses, where it is sold for towing. Cut steel cable with a cold chisel and hammer, a bolt cutter, or a hacksaw.

Cable clamps: Shown above is a U-shaped cable clamp, the most common

type. It is used to hold a loop in the end of a steel cable. Be certain that the cable-clamp saddle is made of heavy steel, and use two clamps on any loop.

Universal joints and swivels: These are used together, at different points, to make a horizontal tire swing that will move in any direction without twisting the chains (page 2347). Shown above, left, is a heavy-duty universal joint purchased at an army-navy surplus store. It has a grease fitting attached to the center, which permits easy, thorough lubrication. To prepare the device for use, a threaded rod has been welded to the top yoke, and a cotter-pin clevis bolt has been welded to the bottom yoke. In the center is a universal joint made for an automobile. It lacks both the grease fitting and the strength of the first, but is adequate for backyard use. At right, above is a utility company swivel. This is what permits a tire swing to spin like a top, without the chains getting twisted. It should not be used in place of the universal joint at the top of the swing; it is used lower down, where there is less wear and abrasion (Figure D, page 2348).

Tires: Both regular and giant tires, worn beyond vehicle use, are available at little cost from tire dealers, recapping services, trucking contractors, and heavy construction contractors.

Utility poles: Unfortunately, utility poles, which make excellent anchor posts when trees are scarce, are becoming scarce themselves. If you are persistent, you may be able to get a used one from a utility company.

Betty Park is a teacher whose interest shifted from painting to woven forms when she discovered the pleasure of working with wool, linen, jute, silken threads, and heavy ropes, and the many ways they can be bound together. Betty also found that her friends could not resist putting their arms through her woven constructions, and this prompted her to make swings. She began with swings for babies, but soon moved on to larger structures that adults can curl up in (page 2357).

Weaving, Braiding, and Knotting
Baby swing

$ ⌛ 👤 🦎

The indoor swing pictured opposite is designed for use by babies weighing up to 30 pounds. Its strength is in the ¼-inch-thick support ropes, which are covered with decorative, brightly colored yarns. These directions are for a swing that will be suspended from a 7½- or 8-foot-high ceiling, but you can easily make the support ropes longer or shorter if your ceiling is of a different height. Keep the seat of the swing within 15 inches of the floor.

Materials
To make the swing you will need: a metal ring 9 inches in diameter and strong enough to support the child's weight without bending (for the seat); 40 feet of ¼-inch-thick manila or nylon rope (for the supports); seven 2-ounce skeins of 3-ply rug yarn or a comparable amount of yarn of varying weights, one color or a mixture (for covering the supports); one 4-ounce skein of knitting worsted; one ball of 3-ply jute; a cushion measuring approximately 11 by 14 inches; and one or more small bells (optional). To suspend the swing from the ceiling, you will need a solid brass ring 1¼ inches in diameter and a porch-swing-size metal screw hook. (Brass rings and 9-inch metal rings are sold in craft supply stores; the 9-inch rings are also available by mail from Creative Fibers, 1028 E. Juneau Ave., Milwaukee, Wisc. 53202.)

To Make the Swing
Turn the porch-swing hook well into a ceiling beam or rafter over the point you want the swing to be. Slip the 1¼-inch brass ring over the hook. Cut off 1½ yards of the ¼-inch rope; set this aside until later. For the support ropes, cut the remaining 35½ feet of ¼-inch rope in half, and draw both pieces through the brass ring until all four ends are touching the floor.

Cut a 1-yard length of jute. If necessary, untangle the four support ropes; then gather them into a bunch 10 inches from the floor. Wrap and knot the jute around the four ropes to join them at this point (Figure N, page 2356). This binding will bear most of the baby's weight, so it must be very strong.

Next, wrap the 9-inch metal ring with jute (Figure O). Cut four 2-foot lengths of jute and put them aside. Place the jute-wrapped ring inside the four support ropes, just above the knot. Space the support ropes evenly around the ring so the binding is centered under the ring. Make sure the support ropes do not cross each other between the wrapped ring and the brass ring near the ceiling. Push the wrapped metal ring down firmly. Using the 2-foot-long jute ties that you cut, bind the ring to the ropes at the four points where ring and rope touch (Figure P). Then loop each end of the four support ropes back to the ring and tie it there (Figure Q).

Cut six more 2-foot lengths of jute. Form the back and arm rests by tying the remaining 1½ yards of ¼-inch rope to the support ropes with jute at six points (Figure R). Tie all these points loosely at first, so you will be able to adjust the slack in the rope and form equal curves between the points, then tighten the ties. Wrap this framework with rug yarn or other decorative yarn, including those parts of the four support ropes that are between the seat and the arm rests. As you wrap, hide jute ends with the yarn and reinforce binding points. (Cut the rug yarn into 3-yard lengths for easy handling while you wrap.)

For the vertical lengths of decorative yarn that will conceal the support ropes, arrange skeins or balls of rug or other yarn in a box, so five strands can be pulled out simultaneously. Pull a set of strands up through the brass ring at the top and back down to the floor, so that it lies along one pair of support ropes. Cut the yarn at floor level. The yarn hanging below the swing seat will be used to make tassels. If you like, pull additional sets of five strands through the ring, cutting the yarn when it reaches the floor, until the support ropes are concealed to your satisfaction (about 15 or 20 strands total). Do the same with the other pair of support ropes. If you are using more than one color of yarn, twist the yarns around the ropes and each other for color variation.

Next, cut twenty 30-inch lengths of knitting yarn and fold each in half. Use these

Thirty-month-old Liz enjoys the color, texture, and tinkling bells of this yarn swing. Betty Park has made a large number of these swings, which can be used to display hanging plants when children outgrow the swings. The side view of the yarn swing shows how the back and arm rests are made of rope, wrapped in yarn, to keep the swinger secure.

doubled lengths of yarn to bind the decorative yarns to the support ropes at 1-foot intervals. Using 3-yard lengths of knitting yarn, bind the decorative yarns to the back support ropes solidly for 5 inches above the back rest. Then use the same yarn to bind the decorative yarns to the two front support ropes, beginning at the ring and ending 7 inches above the arm rests. To make the tassels, cut four 36-inch lengths of knitting yarn. Double each length of yarn and bind the decorative yarn ends, just under the wrapped ring. Trim the tassels to an even length (Figure S).

Tie the bell or bells to the wrapped ring. Insert the cushion in the swing, so it rests on the metal ring and bound support ropes. When the child outgrows the swing, remove the cushion and use the swing to hold a plant set in a saucer.

For related entries, see "Hammocks and Slings," "Kites," "Preschool Activities," "Soapbox and Skate Vehicles," and "Tree Houses."

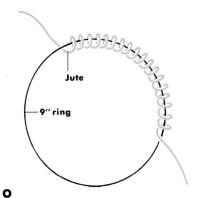

O

Figure O: Cover the metal ring for the baby-swing seat by wrapping it with jute, spiral-fashion. When the ring is completely concealed, knot and trim the ends.

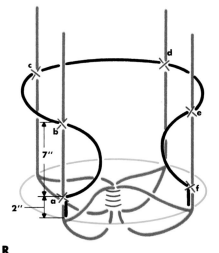

R

Figure R: To make the back and arm rests of the swing, use 24-inch lengths of jute to tie a ¼-inch rope to the support ropes. Placing one end of the rope on a front support rope at ring level, make the first tie 2 inches up (a). Make the second tie 7 inches up from the last, on the same support rope (b). The third tie (c) on the back support rope is slightly higher than b. Proceed to points d, e, and f, making sure the second end of the rope ends at ring level, 2 inches below point f.

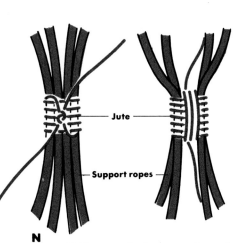

N

Figure N: To secure the four support ropes beneath the seat of the baby swing, wrap and knot a 1-yard-long piece of jute around the ropes, at a point 10 inches above the floor. Wrap the jute first horizontally, and knot it several times (left). Then wrap it vertically and knot the ends together again (right). Alternate these horizontal and vertical bindings until you have used up the yard of jute. Then trim projecting ends to ½ inch.

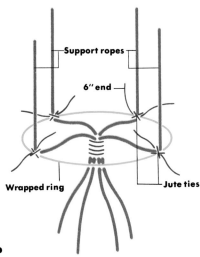

P

Figure P: Use 24-inch lengths of jute to bind the ring to the four support ropes. Wrap and tie the jute repeatedly around the binding points until only 6 inches of each jute tie remains unused.

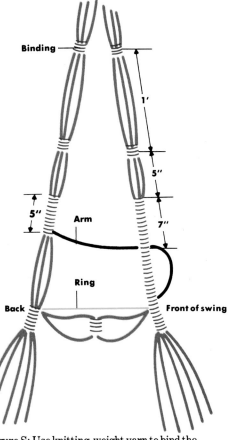

S

Figure S: Use knitting-weight yarn to bind the decorative yarns to the core of support ropes. Do the binding at 1-foot intervals, wrapping the yarn tightly; end with a few knots. At the back of the swing, bind tightly for 5 inches above the back rest. At the front, bind the decorative yarns and the rope together from the wrapped ring to a point 7 inches above the arm rests.

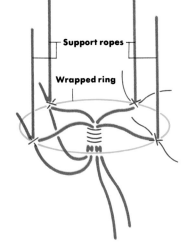

Q

Figure Q: To form a loop with the floor end of a support rope, bring it up to the nearest binding point on the wrapped ring, and secure it with the 6-inch end of jute tie that remains. Wrap and knot as before, until the jute is used up.

This large, woven structure lets an adult rediscover the pleasure of a swing while he is surrounded by soft, beautiful yarns.

Sweetness and Light

Modane Marchbanks, a Georgia native, lives in Englewood, New Jersey. After she was graduated from the University of Georgia, she taught home economics for three years, then became an industrial home economist. She tested and developed recipes, promoted food products and household equipment, and became expert at styling foods. She is now a free-lance home economics consultant, numbering several large food companies as clients.

If you only think of syrups in connection with special dinnertime desserts and lazy Sunday morning breakfasts, you have a pleasant surprise awaiting you. It is true that these sweet, thick liquids are delicious drizzled over pancakes and waffles as well as over ice cream, puddings, cakes, and fresh fruit compotes. But it is equally true that syrups can add a flavorful gloss to a meat roast when used as a glaze, give baked beans a taste zest, or turn a milkshake into a nutritious breakfast-in-a-glass for hurry-up weekday mornings.

Syrup or Sauce?
Syrups and sauces are sometimes confused, but there are three characteristics that set them apart. First, syrups are always made with sugar or sugar-based products, while sauces seldom are. Light can shine through a glass pitcher of any syrup because it will always be translucent, although it may have a clear, rich color. Sauces are opaque by comparison. Finally, syrups never contain particles of ingredients; if solids are used for flavoring, they are strained out before use. But a sauce may contain many such particles.

From a Recipe or a Jar?
It would be difficult to make some syrups at home. Maple syrup is one example, unless you happen to have a grove of sugar maples in your backyard. Chocolate is another, since it is all but impossible to make the syrup from cocoa beans in a home kitchen. Hence, some of the recipes that follow are based on commercial syrups, either used in cooking or mixed with syrups you have made from scratch.

Kitchen Favorites and Celebrations
Beverages and desserts

Quick Fruit-Flavored Syrup
Ingredients:
*1 envelope (.24 ounce) powdered soft-
   drink mix, unsweetened, in any fruit
   flavor*
¼ cup water
1¾ cups light corn syrup

In a tightly covered jar, shake the soft-drink mix and water together. Add the corn syrup and shake until thoroughly blended. Keep covered and store in a refrigerator. Makes 1 pint.

To make an ice-cream soda: Place a scoop of ice cream in a tall glass. Add 2 to 4 tablespoons of chilled fruit-flavored syrup. Fill the glass with carbonated water. Serve with a straw and a long-handled spoon.
   To make a milk bubbler: Pour 2 to 4 tablespoons of syrup into a tall glass, and add 2 tablespoons of milk. Stir until the mixture is well blended. Slowly fill the glass about half full of carbonated water. Stir until mixed. Add 1 scoop of ice cream in any flavor, stirring slowly. Slowly fill the glass to the top with carbonated water.

Remember the deliciously sweet flavor of the ice-cream sodas served at a soda fountain? You can capture that taste treat with fruit-flavored syrups made at home, using the recipe above.

Powdered soft-drink mixes are the basis of these fruit-flavored syrups. From top to bottom they are orange, lemon-lime, and cherry.

Freshly grated nutmeg garnishes a milkshake made with a commercial sorghum-blend syrup.

Mocha-flavored syrup is something different to try when you want to perk up a dish of ice cream.

Syrup-Flavored Milkshake

As a fast breakfast or a late-night snack, a milkshake can be quickly whipped up in a blender. The amount and type of syrup flavoring and the flavor of the ice cream used can be varied to satisfy each individual's flavor cravings.

Ingredients:

½ pint vanilla ice cream
½ cup cold milk
1 to 2 tablespoons commercial syrup
    (maple, cane, or sorghum blend)
Grated nutmeg (optional)

Place the ice cream, milk, and syrup in a blender. Cover and blend at low speed until the mix is smooth and frothy. Pour into a tall glass and sprinkle with freshly grated nutmeg. Makes 1 serving.

Mocha Syrup

This mocha-flavored syrup is a blend of commercial chocolate syrup with coffee syrup made with the recipe below. You can adjust the proportions of the two syrups to suit individual preferences. Start with equal amounts of each; then add more of one or the other to taste.

Coffee Syrup

Ingredients:

3 tablespoons instant or freeze-
    dried coffee
1 tablespoon water
½ cup light corn syrup

In a small saucepan, stir the water into the coffee, dissolving the coffee completely. Next, stir in the corn syrup. Bring the mix to a boil, stirring frequently; then remove from the heat. Let the liquid stand for about 3 minutes; then skim off the foam. This recipe makes about ⅔ cup, but it can be doubled if you like.

Coffee Liqueur (not pictured)

This spirited liqueur can be served as an after-dinner cordial, stirred into hot coffee, or poured over ice cream. A hot-weather drink can be made with equal parts of coffee liqueur, milk, and club soda, whirred together in a blender with an ice cube or crushed ice.

Ingredients:

1¾ cups sugar
3 cups light corn syrup
½ cup instant coffee
½ cup boiling water
3½ cups vodka
1 tablespoon vanilla

In a 3-quart saucepan, mix the sugar and corn syrup and bring to a boil, stirring occasionally. Remove from the heat. Dissolve the instant coffee in boiling water. When the syrup and the coffee reach room temperature, mix them together. (The syrup will be thick.) Add the vodka and the vanilla. Pour the liqueur into hot, sterilized bottles, and tightly cover them with caps or corks. This recipe makes 3½ pints. To enjoy peak flavor, use within three months.

A sweet but tangy lemon syrup and whipped-cream topping turn a cake-mix cake into a festive party dessert.

Fruits of the season can be sweetened and flavored with a topping of anise-flavored syrup.

Fresh Lemon Syrup

Tangy but sweet, this lemon syrup can be poured over a piece of unfrosted white cake topped with whipped cream to make a type of cottage pudding. The syrup can also be used in beverages.

Ingredients:

½ cup light corn syrup
½ cup sugar
⅔ cup water
2 tablespoons grated lemon rind

In a small saucepan, stir the corn syrup, sugar, water, and lemon rind together. Bring the mixture to a boil and boil for 5 minutes. Strain to remove the lemon rind. Cool, and store in a refrigerator until needed. This recipe makes about 1¼ cups of lemon syrup.

Lemon-Syrup Lemonade
(not pictured)

Single serving: In a tall glass, mix 2 tablespoons of lemon syrup, 2 tablespoons of lemon juice, and ⅔ cup of cold water. Add ice cubes and garnish.

Twelve servings: In a large pitcher, stir together 1¼ cups of lemon syrup, 1¼ cups of lemon juice, and 5 cups of cold water. Add ice cubes and garnish with lemon slices. This recipe makes about 2 quarts (⅔ cup per serving).

Lemon Party Punch (not pictured)

In a large pitcher, stir together 1¼ cups of lemon syrup, ¾ cup of lemon juice, and 2½ cups of water. Just before serving, pour in 1 pint of bottled ginger ale, chilled. Garnish with lemon slices or fruit slices. This recipe makes about 2 quarts or 12 servings, each ⅔ cup.

Anise Syrup

Ingredients:

½ cup water
1 teaspoon anise seed
2 cups sugar
1 cup light corn syrup
Few drops of red food coloring,
    if desired

Place the anise seed in water, and let it stand several hours or overnight. Then place the water-and-anise-seed mixture, sugar, and corn syrup in a small saucepan and bring to a boil, stirring constantly. Boil gently for 5 minutes; then strain to remove the seed. If you so desire, stir in food coloring.

You can serve this syrup over fresh peaches or other fresh fruit compote to add flavor and sweetness. Let it marinate about an hour in the refrigerator before serving.

The Spanish use this anise syrup to flavor Persian melon, cantaloupe, or honeydew melon. Cut a 2-inch-round plug from the bottom of the melon, and remove the pulp and seeds with a spoon. Pour about ½ cup of the anise syrup into the fruit. Replace the plug and shake the melon carefully to distribute the syrup. Place the melon in a plastic bag and refrigerate for several hours. Drain the syrup and set it aside. Cut the melon into wedges, pour on the remaining syrup, and serve.

Anise syrup can be thickened by longer cooking and used as a glaze for freshly baked sweet rolls or breads, a traditional Mexican use. The glaze may be decorated by sprinkling on multi-colored sugar.

Raspberry syrup, made from frozen berries, has been drizzled over a molded *Rote Grütze* topped with unsweetened whipped cream. The pudding is made of raspberries and currants.

Rote Grütze with Raspberry Syrup

This pudding, of German origin, is ideally made with fresh currants and raspberries. Since the season when these fruits are plentiful is short, however, an out-of-season version can be made with frozen raspberries and currant jelly.

Rote Grütze can be molded into a decorative shape. If you prefer a softer consistency, use less of the thickening agent, cornstarch. The pudding is usually served with unsweetened whipped cream topped with raspberry syrup (recipe follows).

In-Season Rote Grütze

Ingredients:
1 *pint fresh currants*
1 *pint fresh red raspberries*
1½ *cups water*
1 *cup sugar*
¼ *teaspoon salt*
¾ *cup cornstarch*
½ *cup water*
1 *tablespoon lemon juice*

Sort and gently wash the fruit; then drain. In a deep kettle or saucepan, place the fruit and 1½ cups of water; cover, bring to a boil, reduce heat, and simmer for 10 minutes. Strain through a fine sieve or cheesecloth. Measure the juice into a kettle, adding water if necessary, to make 2½ cups of liquid.

Add sugar and salt. Heat, stirring constantly, until the mixture comes to a boil and the sugar is completely dissolved. Mix the cornstarch with the remaining ½ cup of water; stir this mixture into the fruit mixture. Bring to a boil, stirring gently but constantly, and boil for 3 minutes. Remove from the heat and stir in lemon juice. Pour into a 1-quart mold or individual molds. Chill thoroughly. To serve, run a table knife around the edge between the pudding and the mold, place the serving dish over the mold, turn them both over, and unmold the pudding. Garnish with unsweetened whipped cream topped with raspberry syrup (recipe follows). 6 servings.

Out-of-Season Rote Grütze

Ingredients:
2 *packages (10-ounce) frozen red*
  raspberries
1 *jar (10-ounce) red currant (or*
  strawberry) jelly
¼ *teaspoon salt*
⅓ *cup water*
⅓ *cup cornstarch*
1 *teaspoon lemon juice*

Place thawed raspberries in a saucepan and bring just to a boil, stirring constantly. Strain through a fine sieve or cheesecloth. Measure the juice, adding water if necessary, to make 2 cups. Pour into the kettle or saucepan. Add jelly

and salt. Cook over low heat, stirring constantly, until the jelly is completely dissolved; then bring to a boil. Mix the cornstarch and water and stir into the fruit mixture. Bring to a boil, stirring gently but constantly, and boil for two minutes. Remove from the heat and stir in lemon juice. Pour into a 1-quart mold or individual molds. Chill thoroughly. To serve, run a table knife around the edge between the pudding and the mold, place the serving dish over the mold, turn them both over, and unmold the pudding. Garnish with unsweetened whipped cream topped with raspberry syrup (recipe follows). 6 servings.

Raspberry Syrup

Ingredients:
2 *packages (10-ounce) frozen red*
  raspberries
1¼ *cups sugar*
2 *tablespoons lemon juice*

Place thawed raspberries in a saucepan, and cook over medium heat until the boiling point is reached. Strain them through cheesecloth or a very fine strainer. Return the juice to the saucepan; add sugar and lemon juice. Bring this mixture to a boil, and cook gently about 15 minutes or until a syrupy consistency is reached. Remove from the heat and skim off any foam. Cover and refrigerate. Makes about 1¾ cups.

The caramelized sugar topping on the flan, a smooth baked custard rich with eggs, coated the inside of the baking dish. More caramel syrup can be poured over individual servings.

Flan with Caramel Syrup

A flan is a baked custard topped with syrup. (In Latin American countries, where it is a popular dessert, coconut milk is used as part of the liquid.) The first step is preparing the baking dish by glazing it with caramel syrup.

Ingredients:

½ cup sugar	½ teaspoon salt
5 large eggs	3 cups milk
½ cup sugar	1 teaspoon vanilla

In a small skillet, melt ½ cup of sugar over medium heat. Stir constantly with a metal spoon until you have a light brown syrup, with all grains of sugar melted. The sugar will lump (photograph 1) before it melts.

Immediately pour this syrup into a 1½-quart baking dish, or divide it into eight 6-ounce custard cups. Tilt to allow the glaze, which hardens quickly, to run up the sides of the dish.

In a large bowl, beat the eggs, remaining ½ cup of sugar, and salt until they are mixed and a pale, creamy color. Gradually beat in the milk and vanilla until all ingredients are well blended. Pour the mixture into the glazed baking dish or custard cups.

Set the dish or cups in a shallow baking pan, and fill the pan with hot water to about 1 inch below the rim of the dish or cups. Bake at 300 degrees Fahrenheit for about 1 hour, or until a knife inserted in the center comes out clean. Cool the flan on a rack; then chill thoroughly in the refrigerator. At serving time, run a table knife around the edge between the dish and the flan to loosen the flan. Then invert the serving plate over the dish, turn both upside down, and unmold. The baked custard will have the caramel syrup on the top and sides. Makes 8 servings.

Caramel Syrup

Cook this syrup until it reaches the thickness desired. For a more pronounced caramel flavor, allow the sugar to brown more, but avoid scorching.

Ingredients:

½ cup sugar	1 cup water

In a heavy cast-iron skillet or frypan, heat the sugar over medium heat, stirring it constantly with a metal spoon until the sugar is melted and caramel-colored. Remove from the heat. Carefully add water. After the mixture stops bubbling, return it to the heat and cook, stirring constantly, until the caramelized sugar is dissolved. The sugar is syrup when bubbles form evenly across the surface of the liquid (photograph 2). Cook about 5 minutes, stirring occasionally, to reduce the syrup to the consistency you desire. This recipe makes about 1 cup. This caramel syrup can also be poured over ice cream or cake.

1: Sugar is caramelized by melting it over medium heat, stirring constantly. It will form lumps before it melts. When the sugar has all melted, it will be a light-brown liquid; be careful not to scorch it.

2: To reduce the melted sugar into a thicker caramel syrup, let it boil for several minutes until bubbles form evenly across the surface.

Uses of honey

Flavors and consistencies of honey made from flower nectar vary greatly; your taste will determine whether you prefer a milder or stronger flavor of honey. Honey can be used as any other syrup—as a sweet spread, in recipes to replace all or part of the sugar, to sweeten beverages, in marinades, or as a glaze for meats and vegetables. In addition, fruit salad dressings are often improved with the addition of a small amount of mild-flavored honey.

Basic sugar syrups

These simple syrups can be used when you can fruit, in place of corn syrups in recipes, or to sweeten fresh fruit.

	Sugar		Water
Thin syrup	¼ cup	to	1 cup
Medium syrup	½ cup	to	1 cup
Thick syrup	1 cup	to	1 cup

Boil the sugar and water for several minutes, or until the sugar dissolves. For canning, you usually need 1 to 1½ cups of syrup for each quart of fruit.

Storage of purchased and homemade syrups

When you store honey, maple syrup, and other commercial syrups, you can safely keep the unopened containers at room temperature. But once the container has been opened, or with any syrup made at home, cover the syrup and refrigerate it to protect it against mold. If crystals form, you can place the container in hot water to dissolve them. Then cover and refrigerate.

Baked beans from a can take on distinctive added flavor from maple syrup and dry mustard stirred into the beans and from bacon strips placed on top.

Kitchen Favorites and Celebrations
Syrup-flavored main dishes   ¢ ▯ 🏃 🍴

Baked Beans with Maple Syrup

This is a simple recipe that uses commercial maple syrup, molasses, or a syrup blend to add flavor to canned baked beans.

Ingredients:

2 cans (16-ounce) of baked beans or pork-and-beans
½ cup maple syrup, molasses, or a syrup blend
1 teaspoon dry mustard
¼ pound bacon or lean salt pork, sliced (optional)

In a bowl, stir together the beans, syrup, and dry mustard. Turn into a 3-quart baking dish. Place strips of bacon or salt pork on top, if desired. Bake at 350 degrees Fahrenheit for 45 minutes or until the bacon is thoroughly cooked and the beans begin to brown on top. This recipe makes 6 servings.

Pork Shoulder Roast with Ginger Syrup Glaze

Ingredients:

One pork shoulder, 5 to 8 pounds
Salt and pepper to taste
Fresh-ginger syrup glaze (recipe follows)

Rub the outside of the meat with salt and pepper. Place the roast, fat side up, on a rack in an open roasting pan. Insert a meat thermometer into the center of the roast, through the thickest part. Do not let the tip of the thermometer touch a bone or rest in fat. Roast at 325 degrees Fahrenheit for 3 to 4½ hours, or until the meat thermometer registers 170 degrees Fahrenheit.

About 30 minutes before the roast is done, brush on fresh-ginger syrup to give the roast a shiny glaze. Brush the syrup on several times, but do not start glazing too early because the syrup will brown quickly in the bottom of the pan.

Allow the roast to cool about 15 minutes before carving. Cover and refrigerate any leftover meat for sandwiches. Makes about 12 servings.

3: Fresh ginger-root slices, lemon juice, sugar, corn syrup, and water are the ingredients for a versatile syrup. Not only a meat glaze, it can be used as a topping for fruit or ice cream, or as a base for a party punch.

4: When you use ginger syrup as a glaze for meat, brush it on several times during the last half hour of roasting time.

A syrup glaze made from fresh ginger root gives a hint of oriental flavor to a pork shoulder roast. Ginger slices and parsley are attractive garnishes.

Fresh-Ginger Syrup

Ingredients:

4 *ounces fresh ginger root, scraped*
and sliced
3 *cups water*
2 *cups sugar*
1 *cup light corn syrup*
¼ *cup lemon juice*

In a 2-quart saucepan, place ginger root, water, sugar, corn syrup, and lemon juice. Bring the mixture to a boil over low heat, and cook gently for about 30 minutes. Strain. If you so desire, reserve the fresh ginger slices to use later as a garnish for the roast. This recipe makes about 1½ pints.

This syrup can be used as a glaze for meats, as a base for drinks, or as a topping for desserts.

Sid Sackson has been fascinated by table games for as long as he can remember. He was a civil engineer for 30 years, but since his retirement he has devoted most of his time to creating new games. He has more than two dozen published games to his credit, including Acquire, Executive Decision, Sleuth, *and* Totally. *Sid is the author of* A Gamut of Games *and* Beyond Tic Tac Toe, *and owns a huge collection of games and game books. He and his wife, Bernice, live in New York.*

TABLE GAMES
The Play's the Thing

Have you ever become so engrossed in a game, plotting your next move and anticipating your opponent's, that the outside world ceased to exist? If so, among the projects that follow you should find something new to amuse, challenge, or intrigue you. In each project you will find the rules of a game and directions for making the necessary playing equipment at little cost.

Table games, as such small, portable games are called, are not a contemporary phenomenon. Their roots go back at least 4,000 years to ancient Egypt. Beautifully crafted game boards and playing pieces have been found in tombs. From that time to this, every age and civilization has enjoyed games—either those handed down from one generation to another, or those newly created to fill specific needs.

Why are games so perennially popular? Perhaps because each is a miniature world where all the laws can be understood and mastered. Or perhaps because a game can so absorb the mind that all problems are put aside for a time. Just the fact that winning is fun may be a good enough reason to play.

Most of the games presented here are of ancient origin. The Jungle Game, pictured below and described on page 2370, is a Chinese version of children's chess. Mancala (page 2368) is a game that spread through Africa and Asia with the

Moslem culture, still so popular that in many areas of Africa it is the only game played. Mill (page 2369) originated in Egypt but reached its peak popularity in Europe during the Middle Ages. These games and others are described on pages that follow. One, Quick Trip, is a new game that I designed.

Any of these games can be enjoyed by players of all ages. However, for children I suggest Mancala, Mill, and the Jungle Game. Anagrams, Lasca, and Quick Trip may be more challenging for adults.

Materials

Except for Mancala, any of these games can be played on boards made from ordinary cardboard, but I find that a medium-weight mat board, available in a variety of colors at art supply stores, makes a more durable playing surface. In addition, you will need a ruler, a pair of scissors, and a ruling pen with India ink or a permanent-ink felt-tipped pen. Colored self-adhesive plastic film, available at hardware and art stores, can be used to enhance the designs of the game boards. If you use such plastic, a craft knife with a sharp triangular blade is handy to have for removing the paper backing from small pieces and for maneuvering them into position. Materials needed for a specific game are listed with the instructions for that project. The dimensions given may be altered as you please.

In the Jungle Game, tigers, elephants, wolves, rats, and other animals are pitted against each other on a fanciful board that has traps, dens, and watering holes. The two players pictured are plotting their moves; the one who first moves an animal into the opponent's den will win. Instructions for playing the game and making the game board start on page 2370.

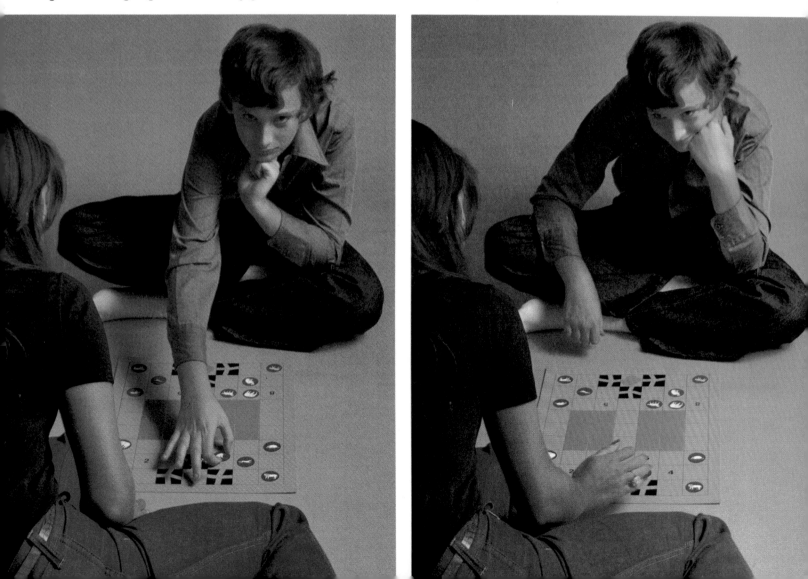

Toys and Games
Mancala

Mancala is a game of capture. Each player in turn removes the playing pieces from one of a series of cups and sows them, one at a time, in other cups around the board. If his last piece ends in a cup containing one or two pieces, the player captures them. Almost unknown to Western civilization, Mancala has been traced to ancient Egypt. The game spread south into Africa and east into Asia. Impromptu games are often played in holes scooped in the ground.

The Game Board
Mancala can be played on almost any surface with two parallel rows of cups. Each row can have six to ten cups when the game is played by two. For the Mancala board (lower left), I used the bottom half of an egg carton. The game could just as well be played in a plastic ice cube tray, a muffin tin, or in jar lids nailed to a board.

Four playing pieces are needed for each cup. African players often use seeds or seashells. The pieces pictured are green glass beads, taken from an old beaded curtain. Marbles, buttons, or even dried beans could be used. Whatever playing pieces you choose, you will need four times as many as the total number of cups in the board. Since there are 12 cups in the egg carton, I used 48 beads.

Rules of the Game
The two players sit opposite each other, facing the game board. Who moves first is decided by tossing a coin or by any other convenient manner. Four playing pieces are placed in each cup. The first player removes all four pieces from any cup on the board and sows them, dropping one piece in each adjacent hole in a clockwise direction (Figure A). As the game progresses, some cups will contain more pieces than others. If the last piece a player sows lands in a cup containing one or two pieces, he captures *all* the pieces in that hole, including the one just sown (Figure B). He removes the captured pieces from the board—to be tallied at the end of the game. As a matter of etiquette, a player is not permitted to remove the pieces from a cup for counting. Once pieces are picked up, they must be sown.

Play continues either until all the pieces have been captured, or until no further captures can be made (Figure C). The player with the most pieces is the winner. If both have the same number of pieces, the game is a tie.

Mancala is played in a thousand different ways and is known by almost as many names. Some of the more familiar are *Wari*, *Awari*, *Chonka*, and *Chisolo*. In one variation, all of the rules remain the same except that a player is permitted to empty only those cups on his side of the board. If, when his turn comes, no pieces remain on his side, his opponent continues playing until he is forced to move one or more pieces to the empty side of the board. In a second variation, not only must a player sow from a cup on his side of the board, he can only capture from a cup on his opponent's side of the board. The player is permitted to sow a last piece in a cup on his side containing one or two pieces, but he does not capture those pieces.

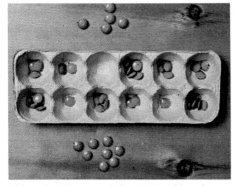

Although Africans craft fine wooden Mancala boards, the game is just as much fun played in any arrangement of 12 to 20 cups fixed in two parallel rows, as in this recycled egg carton. The 48 glass beads came from a beaded curtain.

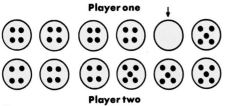

A
Figure A: This is how the Mancala board would look if the first player elected to empty the cup marked with an arrow on his opening move. He sows the pieces one at a time in adjacent cups, always moving in a clockwise direction.

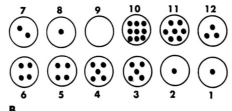

B
Figure B: A capture is made whenever the last piece sown lands in a cup with one or two pieces; all pieces are removed from that cup. If hole No. 1 is emptied, two pieces will be captured at hole No. 2. If hole No. 3 is emptied, two pieces will be captured at hole No. 8. But if hole No. 10 is emptied, three pieces will be captured at hole No. 7.

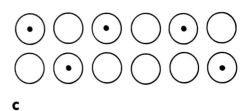

C
Figure C: A 12-cup game of Mancala can end with as many as five pieces left on the board, with no possibility that any can be captured unless one player makes a mistake.

Toys and Games
Mill

¢ ☒ ⅄ 🐁

Mill, also known as Nine Men's Morris, or Merels, is another game that has been traced to ancient Egypt. It reached its height of popularity in Europe during the Middle Ages, where impromptu boards were scratched everywhere, including the seats of cloisters. Played like a complex game of tic tac toe, players attempt to line up markers in rows of three; when one succeeds, he captures an opponent's marker.

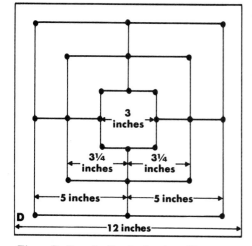

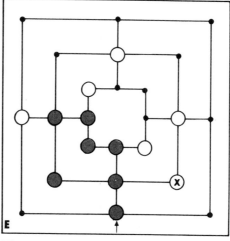

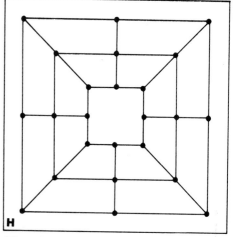

Figure D: To make the simplest board for a game of Mill, enlarge this pattern with a pencil and ruler on a 12-inch square of cardboard. Center a 3-inch, a 6½-inch, and a 10-inch square on the board. Then draw a straight line connecting the midpoint on the edge of each square. Place a dot at the intersection of each line. Darken the playing lines with a felt-tipped marker and you are set to play.

Figure E: To start, players take turns in putting markers on board intersections. As Red enters his seventh marker (arrow) he forms a row of three on a line called a Mill. This entitles him to remove any enemy marker except those already part of a Mill. He chooses the one marked X to prevent White from forming a Mill with his next marker, and to be in a better position to form another Mill.

This board for the game of Mill was made by covering a 12-inch square of cardboard with a 13-inch square of wood-grained self-adhesive plastic, then marking lines with ⅛-inch strips of the same material in yellow. The round dots at the 24 intersections were cut with a ⅜-inch punch and stuck down. The counters are two sets of nine buttons in two colors.

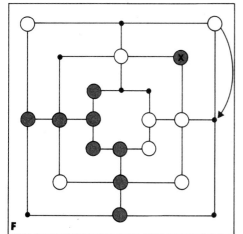

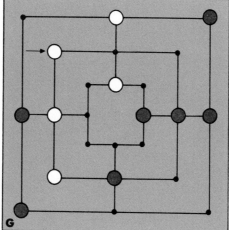

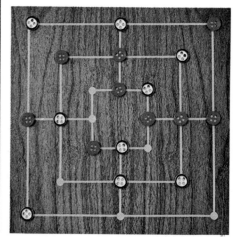

Figure F: The player with white markers moves one down to form a Mill, as indicated by the arrow. But he can only remove the red piece marked with an X, since all other red pieces are already in Mills.

Figure G: Here the white player has established what is called a running Mill. Each time the marker indicated by the arrow is moved to the right or left, a new Mill is formed and another red marker is captured. Red has lost the game.

Figure H: To play a variation of Mill, modify the board to make diagonal Mills possible, as illustrated above.

The board for Mill consists of three concentric squares with four lines joining the sides. To make a quick board, simply enlarge Figure D with pencil and ruler on a 12-inch square of cardboard. Darken the playing lines and mark the intersections with dots, using a felt-tipped marker. To construct a more elaborate board, such as the one shown at right above, you need a 12-inch cardboard square; a 13-inch square of self-adhesive plastic in a dark color (I used a wood-grained pattern); ⅛-inch wide self-adhesive plastic in a light color cut into 16 strips—four each in lengths of 3, 3½, 6½, and 10 inches; and enough self-adhesive plastic in a color matching the strips to cut 24 disks with a ⅜- or ¼-inch punch—to mark the intersections. Cover one side of the cardboard with the dark plastic, notching the excess at the corners so you can wrap the edges to protect them. Use the strips of light plastic to make the concentric squares and to join them (Figure D, page 2369). Use the hole punch to cut 24 disks of light plastic; attach one disk at each intersection of the lines. For playing pieces, I used 18 buttons—nine red and nine white. Checkers, bottle caps, or two kinds of coins could be substituted.

Rules of Play

The board is empty as play begins. Each of the two players receives nine playing pieces of one color. Taking turns, each player puts one of his pieces on any vacant intersection. As a player enters a piece, he either tries to line up three pieces in a row on one line (called a Mill), or he tries to prevent his opponent from doing so (Figure E, page 2369). When a player forms a Mill, he is allowed to remove any one of his opponent's pieces from the board. Once all 18 pieces have been entered, each player in turn moves one of his pieces along a line from the intersection occupied to a vacant adjacent intersection. Whenever a player succeeds in forming a Mill (three pieces in a row), he removes any enemy piece that he wishes except one already part of a Mill (Figure F, page 2369). If all enemy pieces are in Mills, no piece can be removed. The object of the game is to reduce the opposing forces to two pieces, so no Mill can be formed, or to block opposing pieces so none of them are free to move.

A player can move a piece out of a Mill, then back again on a later turn, capturing an enemy piece each time the Mill is re-formed. A player who can set up a running Mill, so that whenever he opens one Mill, he closes another, has a certain victory (Figure G, page 2369).

If both players so agree in advance, the game can be called a draw rather than a win when one player is blocked so he can't move. In one Mill variation that gives an edge to the player who falls behind, the privilege of flying is given when a player is reduced to three pieces. On each of his turns until the end of the game, he can move a piece to any vacant space on the board rather than only to an adjacent space. In another variation, the game is played in the usual manner but the board is made more complex by adding four diagonal lines, connecting the corners of each square as shown in Figure H, page 2369. This creates four additional rows for Mills on the board and the possibility of forming two Mills with one move. When that happens, two enemy pieces are captured.

Toys and Games
Jungle Game

¢ ☒ 🚶 🏌

Although I have not been able to track down the origin of the Jungle Game, I would speculate that it comes from China where it is known as children's chess. As in chess, players start with forces of equal strength, but the pieces have varying degrees of power and their ability to capture other pieces is determined by that power. The object of the game is for one player to infiltrate his opponent's territory and ultimately to occupy his den.

The Game Board

To make a simple playing board for the Jungle Game, enlarge Figure I onto a 14-by-17½-inch sheet of tracing paper, then glue the paper onto cardboard. With a felt-tipped marking pen, darken the lines marking the squares and numbers. Then color the den, traps, and water areas as indicated in Figure I with black, green, and blue pencils, crayons, or markers. To make the playing pieces, trace two sets of the animals shown actual size in Figure K, including the number. Use rubber cement to glue the tracings onto cardboard. Cut out each circle, then color one set of animal pieces red, the other blue. Color lightly so the animal designs are not obscured.

To make a more elaborate board, like the one pictured on pages 2366 and 2367, you will need a 14-by-17½-inch sheet of light green mat board and self-adhesive

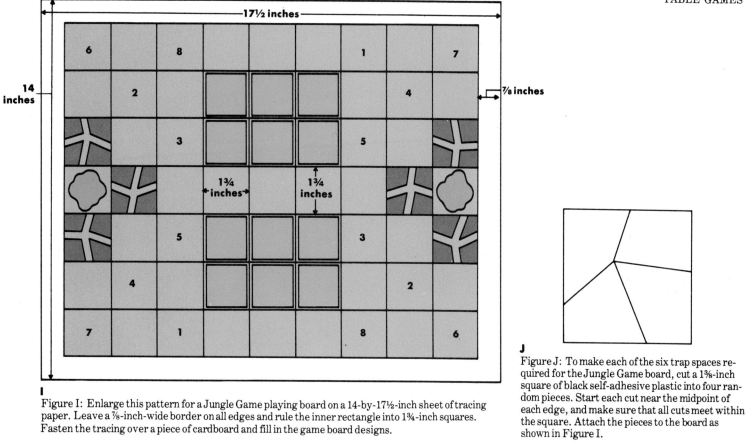

I

Figure I: Enlarge this pattern for a Jungle Game playing board on a 14-by-17½-inch sheet of tracing paper. Leave a ⅞-inch-wide border on all edges and rule the inner rectangle into 1¾-inch squares. Fasten the tracing over a piece of cardboard and fill in the game board designs.

J

Figure J: To make each of the six trap spaces required for the Jungle Game board, cut a 1⅜-inch square of black self-adhesive plastic into four random pieces. Start each cut near the midpoint of each edge, and make sure that all cuts meet within the square. Attach the pieces to the board as shown in Figure I.

K

Figure K: To make the playing pieces, trace two sets of these full-sized patterns. Glue the tracings to cardboard with rubber cement, darken the lines and the numbers with a felt-tipped pen, and color one set blue and the other red. Then cut out the disks with scissors.

plastic in the following colors and sizes: twelve 1 11/16-inch blue squares (water); four 1⅜-inch black squares (traps); and two 1¾-inch dark green squares (dens). To begin, draw a rectangle on the mat board, allowing a ⅞-inch border all around. Divide each edge of the rectangle into 1¾-inch segments. With marking pen and ruler, connect these points to divide the rectangle into 1¾-inch squares. Following the colors in Figure I, fasten the plastic squares to the board, letting the lines between the squares show. Before you put the green squares in place, stack them and round the edges with scissors to make the dens. To create paths in the trap areas, cut each black square into four random pieces, as shown in Figure J. Then align an outside corner of each black piece with a corner of the square. With a marking pen, print numbers 1 through 8 in the spaces, as shown in Figure I.

Battle of the Animals

This is a game for two players. At the start, one player hides a blue playing piece in one hand and a red piece in the other. His opponent chooses a hand to determine the color of the animal army he will command. Then each player, seated behind a den, puts his animal pieces in the spaces marked with corresponding numbers at his end of the board. The player with blue pieces always moves first.

The object of the game is to get an animal piece into the opponent's den. Each player in turn moves one of his animals. A move on land (all spaces except the 12 water spaces) is one space forward, backward, or sideways. Diagonal moves are never allowed. Only the rat can move in and through the water, one space at a time forward, backward, or sideways. A lion or a tiger in a space at the edge of the water can jump straight across, landing in the space directly opposite, provided that it is vacant and that there is no rat, either friend or foe, swimming along the path of that jump (Figure L).

An animal can capture an enemy animal by moving one space forward, backward, or sideways into the space occupied by that animal, but only an animal of the same or lesser power, as indicated by the number, can be captured. There is one exception; the rat can capture an enemy elephant (the Chinese say it does so by crawling into the elephant's ear). A rat leaving the water cannot capture an elephant, however, but one rat can capture the other rat either when entering or leaving the water or when both are in the water or on land.

The trap spaces at both ends of the board can be entered and left freely by any animal. An animal in a trap on its own side of the board is not affected. But an animal in an enemy trap loses all power to resist capture until it moves out of the trap. That animal can capture in the usual way as it enters or leaves the trap, but while it is in the enemy trap, it can be captured by any enemy animal, no matter how weak. A player wins the game by moving any one of his animals into the enemy den. He is not permitted to put any of his pieces into his own den.

Once you become familiar with the rules of the Jungle Game, you might want to try these variations. In one, a lion or a tiger jumping across the water can capture any enemy animal of equal or lower power occupying the opposite square. (In Figure L, the red tiger could capture the blue wolf.) In a second variation, diagonal moves of one space are allowed except when entering the enemy den. All other rules remain the same, and diagonal jumps over water by lions or tigers are not permitted. This variation leads to a faster game but calls for less foresight.

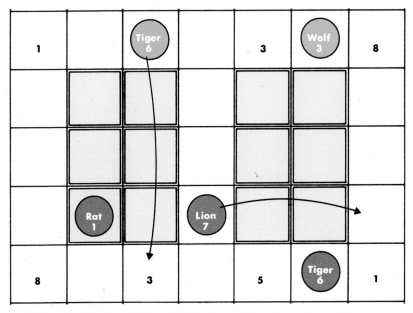

L

Figure L: At this point in the Jungle Game, the blue tiger at the water's edge could jump to vacant square No. 3. The red lion could jump to the vacant space to his right, but not to the left because a rat is blocking the path of that jump. The red tiger could not jump at all because the space opposite is occupied by a blue wolf.

Toys and Games
Anagrams

No one knows where or when letters were first put together to form words just for the fun of it. But there is no doubt that word puzzles are among the best games around.

All you need to play Anagrams is a good supply of letter tiles. The letter distribution shown in Figure M results in a set of 100 tiles. How many sets you need depends on the number of players. If only two people play, one set will suffice; with three or four players, two sets are needed; with five or six, three sets; with seven or eight, four sets. To these minimums you can add as many extra tiles as you want.

To make a set of tiles, you need a 10-inch square of white mat board; metal straightedge; pencil; felt-tipped marker; and craft knife.

With ruler and pencil, divide the mat board into 1-inch squares. Following Figure M, print a letter about ½ inch high in the center of each box with the felt-tipped marker. To protect the tiles, you can cover the back with colored self-adhesive plastic and the front with transparent plastic. Use a craft knife and metal straightedge to cut the tiles apart. Store the tiles in any small container.

Rules of Play

To begin, place the tiles face down on a table and mix them. Move the tiles to one side so the center of the table is clear. One at a time, turn the tiles face up to form a pool of letters. Any player can do this, but he should make sure other players are paying attention as he exposes each new tile. As soon as a player recognizes a word that can be spelled with four or more letters from the pool, he calls out that word. If he is correct, meaning all the letters needed are present and the word is acceptable, he forms the word with those tiles and keeps it on the table in front of him.

It is up to you to set your own house rules on word acceptability. Generally a dictionary is used to settle arguments and proper nouns are not acceptable. Many players like to have a time limit, from 15 seconds to one minute. If no word is called within that time, a new tile is exposed.

If a player calls an incorrect word, the letters remain in the pool and the player is penalized by forfeiting the last word he formed. The tiles of that word are turned face down and mixed back into the pile of unturned tiles. The penalty is waived if the player does not have any words to lose.

A player can also use one or more letters from the pool to steal a word from an opponent. To do this, he must use all of the letters in the original word plus the new letter or letters to form a word with a different meaning (Figure N). Making the word plural or simply adding a suffix is not acceptable. Whenever a player sees a chance to steal a word, he calls out that new word, just as with a word formed from the pool. He is subject to the penalty previously noted if he makes an error. Similarly, a player can add letters to his own words to protect them from theft.

A A A A A A A A
B B
C C C
D D D D
E E E E E E E E E
F F F
G G
H H H H
I I I I I I
J
K
L L L L
M M M
N N N N N N
O O O O O O O
P P
Q
R R R R R R
S S S S S S
T T T T T T
U U U U
V
W W
X
Y Y Y
Z

M

Figure M: Anagrams is played with lettered tiles having this distribution (numbers indicate how many of that letter you should make for each set of tiles). Some letters—N, Z, W, and M—should be underlined to make sure they are read properly even if they are turned on their sides or upside down.

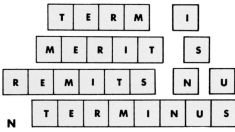

N

Figure N: One of the thrills of Anagrams comes when you can steal a competitor's word. Here, TERM can be stolen by adding an I to form MERIT. Simply adding an S to make TERMS or an ED to make TERMED would not be acceptable; the new word must have a different meaning. With an S, the larceny could continue by turning MERIT into REMITS. REMITS could then be swiped by adding an N and a U to make TERMINUS.

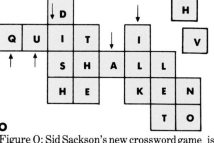

O

Figure O: Sid Sackson's new crossword game is scored this way: All tiles used in two directions count one point each. In this configuration, 13 tiles were used in two directions (all except the five tiles marked by arrows). This nets the player 13 points. In addition, the Q yields a bonus of two points and the K gives a bonus of one point, for a total of 16 points. From this score two points are deducted for each unused tile, making the final score 12 points.

A game of Anagrams can be a raucous affair. If two or more players call out words at roughly the same time, the player with the longer word—whether from the pool or stolen from an opponent—takes precedence. If both words are the same length, a coin can be tossed to decide.

The first player to make seven words is the winner. If no player has that number of words when all of the tiles are exposed, the player with the most words wins. If two players have the same number of words, the player with the most tiles wins.

Variations

In a more genteel form of Anagrams, players politely take turns forming words. To begin, each player turns up a letter. The one with the letter closest to the beginning of the alphabet plays first, and the playing order rotates to the left. The initial letters are returned to the pile face down. Each player in turn draws a letter. If he can use the letter, either with or without letters in the central pool, to form or steal a word, he does so and draws another letter. If he cannot use a drawn letter, he adds it to the central pool and his turn ends.

In a crossword game that I devised using Anagram tiles, any number can play as long as there are enough tiles. One set is ample for four players, two sets for eight.

Each player draws 20 letters. Working with his own letters, each player tries to form words with the highest possible point value that interlock so the words make sense vertically and horizontally, crossword-puzzle fashion (Figure O, page 2373). No letters can adjoin unless they form an acceptable word. If a player draws a letter Q but does not also have a letter U, he is allowed to discard the Q, face up, and take another letter.

Scoring is simple. Most letters that make words in only one direction do not count. Each letter used in two directions scores one point. In addition, certain letters carry bonuses, whether used in one direction or two. The bonus for a J, K, or V is one point, and the bonus for a Q, X or Z is two points. For each of the 20 drawn tiles that are not used, deduct two points from the total score. When the players are finished, the player with the highest score is the winner. Or a set number of rounds can be played and the one with the highest game total wins. To eliminate the luck of the draw, the following procedure can be used. Once the players complete their crossed words, they secretly record them on a sheet of paper. The tiles are then passed to the player on the left, and each player makes a new configuration and records it. This continues until each player has worked with each set of 20 tiles. The player with the highest total score for all the rounds wins.

Toys and Games
Lasca

Lasca is an interesting variation of the familiar game of checkers, invented by Emanuel Lasker, world chess champion from 1894 to 1921. The game board pictured at left was woven by my wife, but you can make one faster by drawing the 2-inch squares on a 14-inch square of cardboard, then coloring them with two felt-tipped markers of contrasting colors. As Figure P shows, there are seven squares of alternating colors on a side and the corner squares must be dark. For playing pieces, I use plastic poker chips because they stack securely; checkers work just as well. You need 11 red pieces and 11 white. You must be able to differentiate between the two faces of each piece. I marked my pieces by punching out ¼-inch disks of black self-adhesive plastic and attaching a disk to one side of each piece.

Rules of Play

The two players use any convenient method of choosing who will command the lighter colored pieces. He will move first. Then each player arranges his pieces with blank faces up, using dark squares at the opposite sides of the board (Figure P). When the blank face is showing, the piece is called a soldier; when the piece is turned so the marked side shows, it is an officer. Soldiers move and jump diagonally forward, just as pieces do in checkers. Officers are allowed to move and jump diagonally forward or backward, the same as a king in checkers. As in checkers,

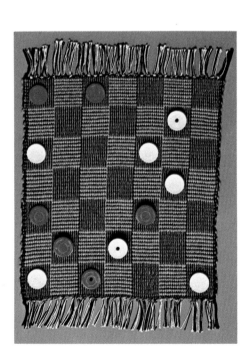

Game boards do not need to be stiff; the Lasca board above is woven of wool yarn. The advantage of a soft game board is that it can be folded up for toting around. In India, chess and pachisi boards are often made of cloth. These playing pieces are red and white poker chips. Unmarked chips represent soldiers; when a soldier becomes an officer, that piece is turned over to reveal the marked side.

jumping opposing pieces is compulsory whenever the opportunity arises.

But what makes Lasca different is this: When a piece is jumped, it is *not* removed from the board. Instead, it is carried along beneath the attacking piece, forming a column (Figure Q). The column is guided by the piece on top and the whole column moves or jumps together, in the same way as a single piece. When a column is jumped, however, only the top piece, known as the guide, is carried along beneath the jumper, leaving behind, freed from captivity, either a single piece or a column with a new guide on top (Figures R and T). When a single soldier reaches the opponent's back row, either by moving or jumping, it is promoted to officer. (Remember to turn the piece over so the mark shows.) When a column reaches the back row, only the guide piece on top is promoted (Figure S). A player's turn ends when one of his soldiers is promoted, even if further jumps are possible (Figure S). An officer that is captured retains its status (Figure T) and may be released later in the game (Figure U). In any series of jumps made by a player during a single turn, the same enemy column cannot be jumped twice (Figure U).

The game is won by the player who captures all of his opponent's pieces or blocks him so he can't move or jump on his turn.

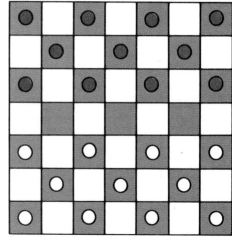

P

Figure P: Lasca starts like a game of checkers. Each player arranges his 11 pieces on the dark squares on his side of the board, with unmarked faces up. A horizontal row in the middle of the board is vacant.

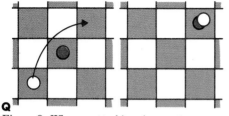

Q

Figure Q: When an attacking piece captures an enemy piece by jumping it, the attacker carries the captured piece beneath it, forming a column. At left, a white soldier jumps a red soldier. The column is guided by the white soldier (right).

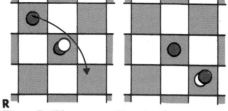

R

Figure R: When an attacking piece jumps a column of two pieces, only the guide piece on top is carried along, freeing the piece below. At left, a red soldier jumps a column, capturing a white guide. This frees the red soldier (right).

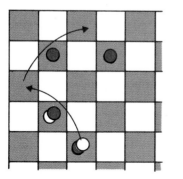
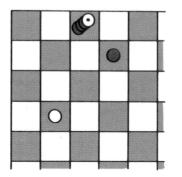

S

Figure S: At left, the column with a white guide can make a double jump over the column with a red guide and a single red soldier. This move frees a white soldier from the bottom of the red column. When the white soldier reaches the end row on his opponent's side of the board, he is promoted to officer and the marked side of the piece is exposed (right). The white player's turn ends with the promotion; the red soldier cannot then be jumped.

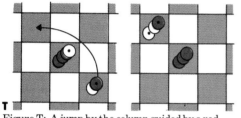

T

Figure T: A jump by the column guided by a red officer (left) carries along the white officer. This results in the arrangement of officers and soldiers in columns at right; the white piece, though captured, does not lose officer status. (In a game, the officer status of the white piece would not show.)

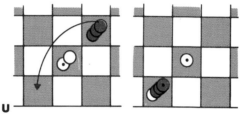

U

Figure U: At left, a red column jumps a column guided by a white soldier to reach white's back row, releasing a white officer. At right, the red guide on top is promoted to officer. He cannot continue by jumping over the white officer, as the same column cannot be jumped twice in one turn.

◯-0	
⬤-1	
◯-2	
◯-3	

V

Figure V: Two movement cards, each measuring 2 by 3 inches, can be cut from a blank 3-by-5-inch index card. On each of 24 movement cards, scribe a row of four evenly spaced ¼-inch circles. From top to bottom on each card, print the numbers 0, 1, 2, and 3 next to the circles (top right). Then color each card with colored pencils, following the color key above.

To assemble a game board for Quick Trip, glue photographs of 12 of your favorite cities on a sheet of heavy cardboard. Connect the cities with a network of colored dots, keyed to match the color of the playing pieces. The objective is to collect points by being the first to land in specific cities when those cities are carrying prize cards.

Quick Trip
¢ ⬛ 🚶 🎮

With memories of past visits abroad and dreams of more to come, I created a racing game that takes place in some of my favorite cities. The game isn't realistic, of course; you couldn't easily make these trips in antique cars like the playing pieces shown on the game board. But it is fun to dream about. If other ports of call have more appeal for you, by all means substitute them.

To make the game board shown at left, below, you will need a 19-by-22-inch sheet of black mat board; an assortment of travel folders; scissors; rubber cement; a black felt-tipped marker; a ⅜-inch hole punch; 6-inch squares of self-adhesive plastic in red, green, blue and yellow to make path markers; and 12 self-adhesive paper labels for marking cities. For game cards you need: 18 blank 3-by-5-inch index cards; a 4-by-4½-inch piece of red mat board; a craft knife; a 12-by-18-inch piece of red and an 8-by-18-inch piece of black self-adhesive plastic. For playing pieces, I used models of four antique automobiles. The markers chosen must indicate the direction of movement and each must match a different color in the paths.

Choose 12 city pictures from the travel folders and position them, following the arrangement shown on the game board. Glue them down with rubber cement. Using a felt-tipped marker, print the name of each city on a paper label. Stick this label beside any edge of the corresponding photograph. For path markers, punch 41 dots each of yellow, red, green, and blue self-adhesive plastic. (The same amount of markers could also be made by cutting the colored self-adhesive into ⅜-inch squares.) Affix a dot in each city; then run a network of paths connecting the cities, using the color pattern shown on the game board. (Instead of punched-out dots, paths can be made of tiny squares or rectangles cut with scissors.)

Three sets of game cards are needed—movement cards, city cards, and prize cards. For the first two, cut two 2-by-3-inch cards from each index card. Cover the back of 24 movement cards with black self-adhesive plastic, and cover the back of 12 city cards with red. Scribe four evenly spaced ¼-inch circles on the front of each movement card. Color and number each circle as shown in Figure V. On the face of each red card, print the name of one of the cities on the game board. For prize cards, cut a dozen 1-by-1½-inch cards of red mat board and print the numbers 4 through 15, one number to a card. Each number represents points scored toward winning the game.

The Traffic Laws

Two, three, or four players can enter the race, each selecting a marker. To set up the game, shuffle the movement cards and place them face down next to the game board. Arrange the prize cards face up in numerical order with No. 4 on top. Shuffle the city cards and deal one to each player. Each places his marker on the city represented by the card he receives. Then return the city cards to the deck and reshuffle it. Place the city cards face down next to the prize cards.

Turn four city cards from the deck face up along one edge of the game board. Starting with No. 4, place a prize card on each of these four city cards. The first player to land—by exact count—in a city with a prize card on it collects that prize card and holds it for scoring at the end of the game. Each time a prize card is won, a new city card is turned up and the next prize card is placed on it. This continues until all 12 city and prize cards have been used. If a player's marker is in a city when that city's card is turned up, the player is not allowed to collect the prize card unless he leaves the city and then returns to it.

For the race to get underway, the player whose marker is in the city closest to the start of the alphabet goes first; then play rotates to the left. Each player in turn draws the top card from the movement deck. He then moves his marker the full number of spaces indicated next to the color that his marker is on at the start of the move. Then he discards the movement card. When all 24 movement cards have been used, reshuffle them to form a new drawing deck.

If a player is in a city at the start of his move, he can leave the city by any path he chooses. But if his marker is on a path, he must continue to move in the direction his marker is pointed. When a movement card indicates "O" movement, the player does not advance his marker but he may, if he wishes, reverse its direction. If a player's move takes him into a city and out again, counting the city as one space, he can leave by any path except the one by which he entered.

When, after the play of a movement card, a marker lands on a space of a matching color, either in a city or along a path, the player draws another card and plays again. He continues until he lands on a space that doesn't match his marker. Markers may pass each other along a path, and two or more markers can occupy the same space.

As soon as the last prize card has been won, the game ends. The player with the highest total value of prize cards wins the race.

Variations

Racing games like Quick Trip are generally quite simple and depend almost entirely on chance—the roll of the dice or the draw of the cards. The variations that follow introduce two more levels of play, the second completely determined by skill. In the first variation, each player is dealt two movement cards at the start of the game. On his first turn, each player uses either one of his cards to move his marker. He then discards the used card and draws a replacement. Thus, he always has two cards to choose between on each turn. In the second variation, at the start of the game each player picks two cards from the movement deck to use throughout the entire game. A player can choose any two movement cards he wishes, except one with a movement of three spaces printed next to the color matching his marker. (If two players want the same card, they toss a coin for it.) On each turn, a player uses either of the two cards. He is permitted to look at the order in which future city cards will be exposed, so he can plan a series of moves. Since the two cards are chosen and not drawn blindly, this variation results in a game where skill is much more important than luck.

For related projects see: "Card Tricks," "Magic," "Piñatas," "Puzzles," and "Toys."

Sid Sackson (left), inventor of Quick Trip, gives playing pointers to some novices. For the duration of the game, the players will travel through the 12 exotic cities pictured on the game board.

TABLES AND BENCHES
Form Follows Function

Of all the things that fill our homes, few are as useful as tables and benches. As a professional wood craftsman, I take special pleasure in making such furnishings, doing my best to keep them both simple and attractive. You can do likewise—and save a pretty penny in the process.

Any of the following projects can be built with hand tools. Power tools, if you have them, will make the work go faster, but not necessarily better. Plywood is the main ingredient in several of the projects, and stock sizes of pine, fir, or cedar are specified. Insofar as possible, the dimensions of the furniture make efficient use of standard materials.

If you are making your first pieces of furniture, the most important elements to watch for are strength, simplicity, usefulness, and attractiveness of design. Wobbly legs, platforms at awkward heights, unnecessary or unsightly structural members, and badly shaped parts are common in homemade furniture, but they can be avoided. If problems like these are dealt with in the planning stage, good results are virtually assured. For the pieces pictured, you can use the exact dimensions and building techniques given here, or you can adapt them for use in designs custom-tailored to the needs of your home.

Furniture and Finishes
A sawhorse stool

A scientist turned woodworker, Harry Remde works with his wife, Gladys, an artist and potter, in historic Morristown, New Jersey, where they design furniture and art for homes and churches. Work of the Remdes has been displayed at numerous exhibitions, including fairs of the American Crafts Council. Harry is the author of The Art in a Craft, *published by Traditional Studies Press, Toronto.*

Left: A bench strong enough to use as a step stool is as easy to build as a sawhorse, and in this case looks a bit like one. A basic notched joint, glue, and nails hold two pairs of 2-by-4 legs on the ends of a 4-by-6-inch timber. The seat shown is 15 inches long but it could be as long as you want to make it.

Opposite: In his workshop, Harry Remde applies the finishing touches to a teak coffee table that he made. The central panel is a tile inlay with a zodiac motif, designed by his wife, Gladys. As he works, Harry sits on a sawhorse bench; instructions for making it begin on page 2380.

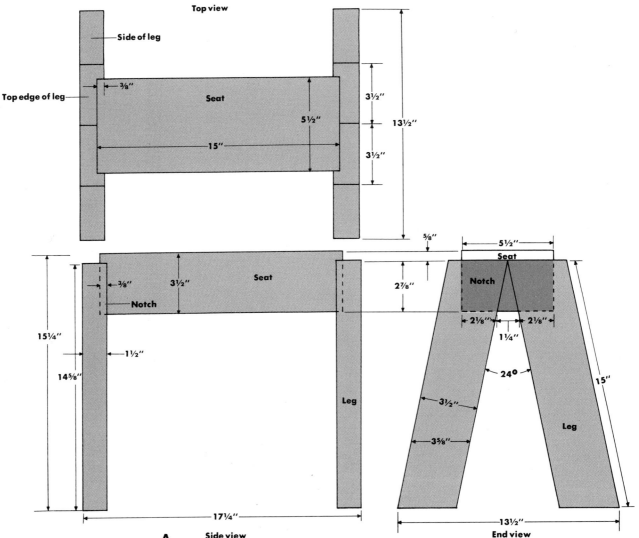

A Side view   End view

Figure A: Above are three views of the sawhorse stool, with actual dimensions. The end view (lower right) shows the position of the rabbet notches (red) that are cut in the legs to hold the seat. These notches are cut with a mallet and chisel to a depth of ⅜ inch.

For a strong but gracefully styled bench, the sawhorse stool shown on page 2379 would be hard to surpass. I designed and made a pair of these in one evening when I realized the night before a crafts show that my wife and I would have no place to sit. A stool this height—15¼ inches—provides useful low seating, and can also serve as a kitchen step stool. The structural lumber used for the seat is strong enough so the bench can be almost any length that is not too heavy to move around.

Materials and Construction
To make the seat shown, you will need 6 feet of 2-by-4 lumber such as fir or cedar (four pieces 16 inches long will do) and a 15-inch or longer piece of 4-by-6 lumber. Also needed are: crosscut saw; mallet and chisel; white glue and bar clamps; try square; rule and pencil; hammer; 16-penny finishing nails; nail set; wood-filler compound; and sandpaper. If the 4-by-6 is the right length with square, smooth ends (it can be purchased in this condition at millwork lumberyards), it will require no further preparation. All the work will be done on the legs, which will be notched to provide a resting place for the seat. The legs I used were 15 inches long, but you can make them any length you want. The important factor is the angle at which they meet. I chose the angle shown (Figure A) for appearance and rigidity; then, measuring, I found it to be 24 degrees. Any angle within a few degrees of this would work, but a much smaller angle would make the bench tend to topple and a much

1: To cut a leg for the sawhorse stool at the proper angle, draw a pencil guideline across the board first. Measure as shown in Figures A and B. Be sure to keep the saw blade at a right angle with the face of the leg as you cut; it helps to extend the pencil line, using a square, down the edges of the board. The backsaw pictured, which has a stiffening strip along the top edge, is very accurate, but a standard crosscut saw could be used.

2: Cut the notches for the seat by tapping a chisel vertically into the wood along the pencil outline to form a stop, then flaking away small chips with the chisel held at the angle shown. When flaking, the beveled edge should face the wood; when forming a stop, keep the beveled edge to the inside of the outline. Note that the ⅜-inch depth of the notch has also been marked with a pencil. The board can be held in place with C-clamps.

3: After brushing white glue on the surfaces to be joined, hold the assembled bench together with bar clamps, as shown, while the glue dries overnight. Put scraps of wood between the clamp heads and the bench so as not to mar the legs.

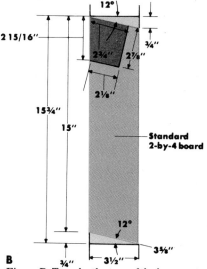

4: When the glue has dried, remove the clamps and drive several 16-penny finishing nails through each leg and into the ends of the seat.

larger angle would make it prone to collapse. To obtain the 24-degree angle, you can simply follow the dimensions given in Figure B. If you prefer, use a protractor to mark the ends of each leg at 12 degrees less than a right angle or 78 degrees. Cut off the ends of each leg (photograph 1), making sure the cuts are parallel. Once all four legs are cut to size, draw a line across the end of the 4-by-6 seat, ⅝ inch below and parallel to the longer edge. Position two of the legs with their ends flush against this line so they meet at the center (Figure A). Trace the outline of the 4-by-6 onto the legs, as shown in dashed lines in Figure A. Alternatively, draw the outline of the shape shown in red in Figure B, following the dimensions given. But tracing the 4-by-6 is likely to be more accurate. Do the same with the second pair of legs. Be sure the four legs form mirror-image pairs.

Notching the Legs

The notch that you have marked on each leg must be chiseled away to a depth of ⅜ inch to give the seat a solid resting place. Cut each notch with a mallet and chisel. First tap the chisel straight down along the pencil lines, flat side facing away from the notch, forming grooves about 1/16 inch deep. Then, flat side up, gradually flake away bits of wood from the surface, holding the chisel at an angle (photograph 2). Work from the end of the board toward the cross-grain groove, which acts as a stop. Work in the direction that the wood grain runs as much as possible. Gentle taps and small bites of wood work best. Measure the depth of the notch from time to time, and continue grooving and flaking until you have made a smooth, flat notch that is a uniform ⅜ inch deep.

Attaching the Legs

To join the 4-by-6-inch seat and the legs, brush a heavy coat of white all-purpose glue into the leg notches and on the corresponding parts of the seat. Assemble the bench by clamping the legs in place (photograph 3). Use scraps of wood to keep the bar clamps from marring the legs. Check with a try square to make sure the legs and the underside of the seat form right angles. If an angle is not quite accurate, adjust it by raising or lowering the position of the clamp head on the leg. Changing this pressure point opens or closes the angle slightly. Let the glue dry overnight; then remove the clamps. For added strength, drive several 16-penny finishing nails at a slight angle through each leg into the seat timber (photograph 4). With a hammer and nail set, drive the nail heads slightly below the wood surface, and fill the holes with wood-filler compound.

Sand the finished bench, rounding all corners and eliminating splinters. You can paint it a bright color with high-gloss enamel, or leave it unfinished, as I did, to emphasize the rustic simplicity.

B
Figure B: To make the tops of the legs meet at a 24-degree angle, as shown in Figure A, draw parallel cutting guidelines, top and bottom, each 12 degrees off square. You can measure this with a protractor or simply duplicate the dimensions indicated above. The area to be notched, again shown in red, can also be marked. It must be square with the angled end, not with the sides of the board.

Furniture and Finishes
A plant table

$ ◪ ⚠ ✈

The short-legged, slat-topped table shown below is designed to be strong enough to hold a heavy load of potted plants. It is made entirely of stock 1-by-3-inch lumber (less than 50 running feet in all are used). You also need: a box of 6-penny finishing nails; a hammer; a rule; a try square; C-clamps; sandpaper; exterior paint; and two saws—one for the crosscuts (across the grain of a board) and one for ripping (making lengthwise cuts). Gluing and clamping are optional but recommended if the table will hold heavy objects.

Construction

To make the rectangular frame onto which the cross slats will be nailed, cut two pieces of wood 40 inches long and two pieces 26½ inches long. Arrange the pieces on edge to form a rectangle with the longer pieces lapping over the shorter ones. Fasten each corner by driving two 6-penny nails through the longer pieces into the ends of the shorter ones. (Blunt the nail points with a hammer to forestall splitting the wood.) Do not worry about rigidity or exact squareness—this will come as the work proceeds. Next cut the 11 slats, each 28 inches long, and nail them to the top of the rectangular frame (Figure C). Nail on the two end slats first, making each flush with the three frame edges. Two nails in each end followed by five or six along the outer edge will secure each end slat. As you nail, check to see that the large rectangle is square. Nail the nine remaining slats onto the top of the frame, spacing them evenly about 1¼ inches apart and using two nails at each end.

5: To make a lengthwise cut in wood, a cut that follows the grain or is at a slight angle to it, use a ripsaw. Clamp the wood lengthwise along the edge of your workbench, and be sure the pencil guideline is outside both bench and clamp.

Gardeners like a slat-topped table for potted plants, since the slats let air circulate and excess moisture drain away. Since this one is made of stock lumber that might rot, it is protected with two coats of exterior paint. Some woods, notably redwood and cypress, are naturally rot-resistant and do not require paint, even when they are exposed to the weather.

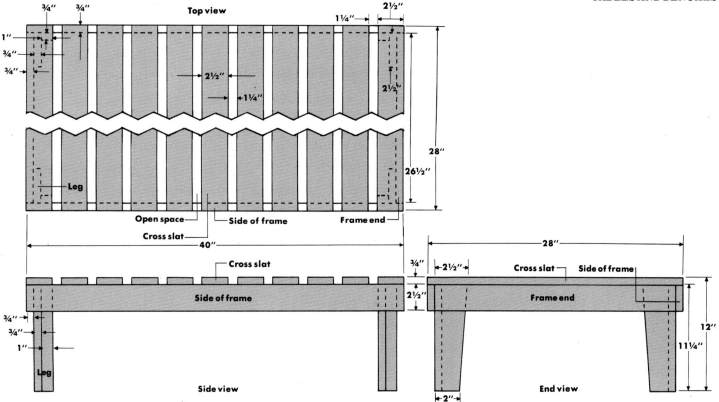

C

Figure C: These drawings of a slat-topped plant table show the size and spacing of all parts. Stock 1-by-3-inch lumber (which actually measures ¾ by 2½ inches) is the only wood used, and only in the legs is it not used in its standard width. Nails are the only fasteners required, but the table can be strengthened with glued joints.

Legs

To make the two-piece legs, first cut six pieces of wood 11¼ inches long. Use the ripsaw to cut two of them into four pieces each 1 inch wide. (A ripsaw is designed to cut best in the direction the grain runs.) Taper the other four pieces from their full 2½-inch width at one end down to a 2-inch width at the other (Figure C and photograph 5). Assemble the legs as shown in Figure D, and sand or plane them smooth and flat where they will join. Since the legs will be strengthened when they are attached to the frame, four nails driven through each large piece into each small piece are adequate for a good joint. Gluing and clamping before nailing are optional, but will give added strength. Next, place each leg in an inside corner of the frame with its top butting against an end slat. The tapered half of the leg goes on the short side of the frame. Clamp the leg in position, check for squareness, and drive three nails from each side of the outer corner through the frame and into the leg. Again, gluing and clamping before nailing are optional but desirable.

Sand the finished plant table and protect it from moisture with two coats of exterior paint.

Design Hints

The simple slat table demonstrates several basic design principles that you can apply to other projects. If nails alone are used for joining boards, a three-way meeting of boards at the corners adds strength. Lining up the narrow sides of the legs with the inner edge of each end slat improves the appearance enough to make ripping the boards worthwhile. Tapering one side of each leg gives visual lightness to the otherwise rectangular structure.

Length, width, and height are also aspects to weigh in advance. Ideal dimensions are often dictated by necessity; the plant table had to be about a foot high (to raise the plants enough so they could get light indoors) and the length and width were determined by economical use of wood on hand. But where a choice is possible, plan overall dimensions in a 3-to-5 or 5-to-8 ratio. No one knows exactly why these relationships work so well, but most designers like to use them.

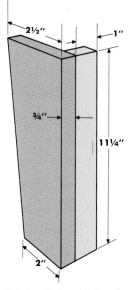

D

Figure D: This detail of a table leg shows how the wider, tapered side laps the narrower, straight one. The taper runs from 2½ inches (the full width of a 1-by-3) at the top to 2 inches at the bottom. Two legs should be constructed exactly as shown above. For the other two legs place the narrower, straight side to the left of the tapered one forming a mirror image.

Furniture and Finishes
Modular tables and benches $ ● ⋔ ✈

If you occasionally need a good amount of extra dining space, or if you need an inexpensive but sturdy place to display your crafts or hobbies, a set of modular tables and benches like those shown below will satisfy the need. Tables like these can be made in sets of three because each top requires exactly one third of a standard 4-by-8-foot sheet of ⅝-inch plywood. (The remainder of any one table is made from three 10-foot lengths of 1-by-3-inch wood, 8 feet of 5/4-by-4-inch wood, and 6 feet of ¼-by-1⅝-inch lattice strips.) Each bench can be made from a single 10-foot length of 5/4-by-12-inch board. (As with other lumber, the nominal dimension is larger than the actual dimension; a 5/4-inch board is a bit thicker than 1 inch, a 12-inch board is 11¼ inches wide.) Select plywood and lumber free of knotholes and other imperfections. In addition to the tools and fasteners used in the previous projects, you will need: 6- and 10-penny finishing nails; eight 2-inch flat-head machine screws, washers, and nuts per table; a drill with countersink bit to match; and paint.

You can finish the tables and benches with bright high-gloss enamels or flat paints in muted tones, depending on your preference. If you make two benches per table, you can seat two adults or three children on each bench.

These tables can be arranged in rows, in blocks of four, five, or six, or in more imaginative patterns such as asterisks or triangles. Because the legs are bolted to the tops, the tables can be dismantled and stacked for storage. One table is drawn in Figure E; I made six tables and 12 benches to seat 24 people at a recent crafts seminar that my wife and I conducted. When the participants went home, we found so many other uses for the tables that we have yet to dismantle and store them.

Modular tables—three tops from a 4-by-8-foot sheet of plywood, and matching benches (one from a 10-foot board)—are an economical answer to a common dilemma: the need for more working or dining space. Sturdy, lightweight, and easily stored, the set pictured is arranged in T-formation for a backyard pottery sale. Bolted legs disassemble in minutes.

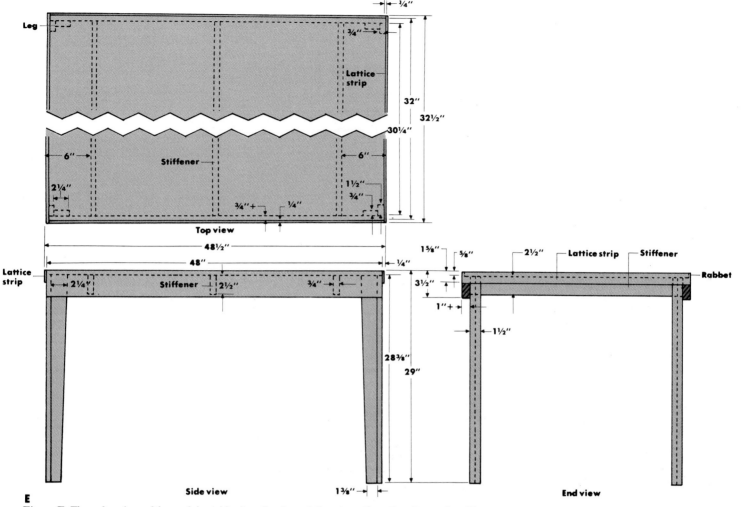

E

Figure E: These drawings of the modular table show the sizes of all parts and how they fit together. The plywood top is edged all around and is stiffened from below with three cross-pieces. Tapered L-shaped legs are attached to the side pieces of the tabletop with machine screws and nuts, so the unit can be disassembled for storage. The area in red is detailed in Figure F.

Assembling the Tabletops

For a set of three tables, saw a 4-by-8-foot sheet of ⅝-inch plywood into three equal parts, each measuring about 32 by 48 inches. Cut the panels with a sharp, fine-toothed crosscut saw, working from the top side to minimize visible splintering, or if you have access to power tools, use a saber saw or a plywood blade in a circular saw. Next, cut two 48-inch lengths of 5/4-by-4-inch lumber to edge the long sides of the tabletop. To make a secure joint that will conceal the layers of the plywood edge, you will need to notch the full length of one edge of each board. This will give the tabletop a small ledge to nest in (Figure F). The notch, called a rabbet in woodworking terms, needs to be ⅝-inch deep (the thickness of the plywood) and a little more than ¾ inch wide, leaving ¼ inch of the board's original thickness to cover the plywood edge. Such a notch can be made in a number of ways. Using a mallet and chisel, as in the sawhorse stool project (page 2381) is possible but very laborious and time-consuming. The best hand tool for this job is called a rabbet plane. It has a blade that extends as far as the tool's side edge, permitting the gradual formation of a sharp inner corner. You use it like any other plane, with the board being notched clamped in a vise. Mark the area to be planed clearly on the board's edge. To keep the plane from wandering on the first sweeps, a guide, either built into the plane or attached to the edge of the board, is necessary. It is much faster and easier, of course, to cut the long rabbet on a circular saw or with a power router.

After rabbeting the two side boards, cut to size three 1-by-3-inch stiffeners for each tabletop. They will measure about 30¼ inches long. These are placed under the tabletop and between the side pieces for stability. Working upside down,

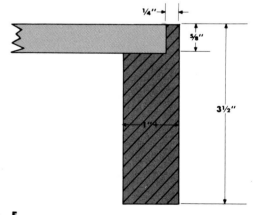

F

Figure F: The rabbet used to fasten the longer and stronger side pieces (shown in red in Figure E) to the tabletop is ⅝ inch deep, matching the thickness of the plywood top. The projection that hides the plywood edge is ¼ inch wide, making the rabbet a little over ¾ inch wide.

6: When flat-head machine screws are used for assembly, as in the tables pictured on page 2384, the countersink bit demonstrated above lets the tapered heads fit flush with the wood surface. Similar bits (called rose bits) are available for use with a hand brace.

assemble the top, the two side pieces, and the three stiffeners as shown in Figure E, page 2385, testing them for squareness and fit. Place one stiffener across the center of the table and the other two 6 inches from either end. Make any adjustments needed with sandpaper, a plane, or a saw. Glue all six pieces together, clamping the side pieces with bar clamps at the three stiffeners. Insert scrap boards the length of the table between the clamp heads and the table edge to distribute the pressure evenly. Let the glue dry overnight. Then remove the clamps and drive pairs of 10-penny nails through the side pieces and into the ends of the stiffeners.

To cover the short sides of the tabletop, cut two 32½-inch lengths of ¼-by-1⅝-inch lattice strip, and fasten them as shown in Figure E, page 2385. File or sand off the edges if necessary. Glue, then nail the strips in place driving eight or ten 6-penny finishing nails through each, into the edges of the top and side pieces. Clamping is not essential, but if you have enough bar clamps, the gluing (though not the nailing) can be done while the other sides are still drying.

The Table Legs

While you are waiting for the glue to dry on the tabletop, you can work on the legs, which are assembled independently. Each leg is made from two lengths of 1-by-3-inch wood. Assuming you want a table height of a standard 29 inches, cut eight pieces, each 28⅜ inches long. For the best appearance, these will need to be cut lengthwise, a time-consuming job if you do not have power equipment. You may want to have these cuts made at the lumberyard, a service most will provide for an additional charge. To match the design pictured, four of the boards need to be cut lengthwise to a width of 1½ inches. (Standard 1-by-2-inch boards could also be used.) The other four should be tapered from a 2¼-inch width at the top to 1⅝ inches at the bottom. These cuts can be made most easily with a saber saw or circular saw. Alternatively, the tapers can be ripped with a hand ripsaw, then smoothed with a hand plane.

Each leg consists of one tapered board and one untapered board, joined at a right angle as shown in Figure E. Sand or plane both pieces smooth and flat on the surfaces where they will join. Glue and clamp; then nail the four leg assemblies, as described on page 2383 and shown in Figure D, but this time let the straight board overlap the tapered one.

To simplify construction, you can eliminate the tapering and ripping of the leg parts. But if you follow the dimensions given, you will make a better-looking table.

Attaching the Legs

To permit easy dismantling and storage, bolt the legs to the tabletop. (If you plan to leave the table standing, you can attach the legs with glue and nails as described on page 2383.)

Bolt the legs to the long side pieces of the tabletop assembly. I used two 2-inch flat-head machine screws, size 10-24, for each leg. To locate the holes at each corner, mark points at 2 and 3½ inches on a diagonal line from the upper corner of the side piece. Drill these holes at each corner, eight in all, using a 3/16-inch bit. Then use a countersink bit so the head of the machine screw can be drawn down flush with the wood's surface (photograph 6). With the tabletop upside down, hold each leg in turn in the corner it will occupy (Figure E, page 2385). Be sure each tapered side is on the long side of the table. Set the leg firmly in the corner and drill matching bolt holes through the legs. Fasten the legs to the tabletop with machine screws, washers, and matching nuts.

The Benches

Simple, sturdy benches like the ones shown on page 2384 are useful, whether or not you make the modular tables, but the dimensions given are calculated so the benches can be used with the tables.

For each bench, you need a 10-foot length of 5/4-by-12-inch lumber, actually 11¼ inches wide. If this kind of wood is not available, you can also make these benches of 10-inch lumber. From the 10-foot board, cut four pieces, one 48 inches long for the seat, two 16 inches long for the legs, and one 36 inches long for a cross strut that will be located under the seat (Figure G).

The bench can be made with rectangular boards, but I think this produces too square a shape. Slight modifications make a big difference in the appearance. Use a

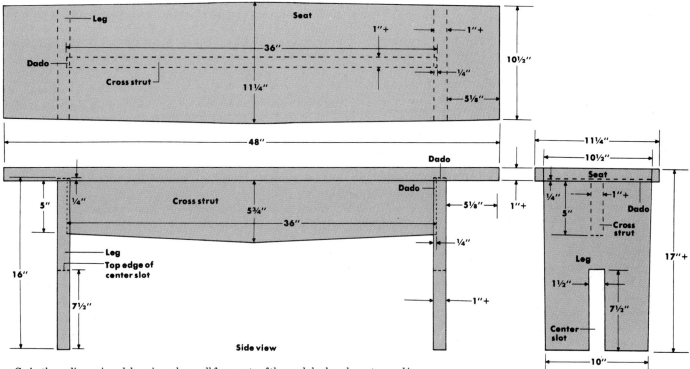

G

Figure G: As these dimensioned drawings show, all four parts of the modular bench are tapered in some way from the original rectangular shape, giving the bench a gently sculptured appearance. Four dadoes—shallow grooves into which the edges of boards fit—make it possible to assemble the parts with glue alone (though hardware fasteners will make a stronger joint). The cross strut is first fitted into the legs and glued, then the legs are fitted into the bench top.

plane and sandpaper to shape the bench top so it tapers slightly toward both ends, as shown in Figure G. The full 11¼-inch width is retained only at the center, with both ends tapering to 10½ inches. Similarly, when you cut the legs, taper them from 10½ inches at the top to 10 inches at the bottom. To create a four-legged look, cut a center slot at the bottom of each leg, 1½ inches wide and 7½ inches high. The long cuts can be made with a ripsaw, then the piece removed with mallet and chisel. Finally, shape the cross strut, making it 5¾ inches wide at the center and 5 inches wide at either end. In this case, the entire taper is made on the lower edge since the upper edge will be butted flush against the bottom of the seat.

Once the four pieces are the proper size, the bench could be assembled by simply butting the pieces together and joining them, first with glue and clamps, then with reinforcing nails or screws. But if you have taken time to shape each piece, you may want to assemble the bench with a further refinement of cabinetmaking—dadoes, which are narrow grooves into which the joining edges fit snugly for gluing. Well-made dadoes strengthen joint construction. Cutting the three-sided channels, ¼ inch deep, can be done with chisel and mallet, but it is a laborious, time-consuming task that demands painstaking care. Dadoes can be cut accurately and speedily with a powered portable dado cutter or with a dado-cutting attachment on a circular saw. The four dadoes should be cut the exact width of the lumber you are using. Locate two of them on the underside of the bench seat, 5⅛ inches in from either end and running the full width of the board. Center the other two on the insides of the bench legs, running from the top edge down to a point 5¼ inches below it. Test the assembly for squareness and fit, attaching the legs first to the cross strut and then to the seat. Make any adjustments that are necessary with sandpaper, rasp, plane, or saw. Spread glue in the dadoes and on the edges that fit into them, reassemble the bench, and clamp the joints while the glue dries.

Finishing
Sand each table and bench lightly. Be sure that no splinters or rough edges protrude. But avoid oversanding the plywood tabletop; sanding may produce ripples that will show through paint, especially if the wood is fir. Dust the surfaces carefully; then apply paint.

TABLES AND BENCHES

Furniture and Finishes
Nesting tables

For those who enjoy a truly challenging project in fine woodworking, the set of nesting tables pictured below is a real test of craftsmanship and ingenuity. A puzzle of sorts, this set of five tables can be condensed into a single neat cube (if you know the combination, as detailed in Figure I, opposite).

For this project, it is advisable to follow precisely the dimensions given. The relationships between parts are so complex that any changes are likely to create unexpected problems.

Tools and Materials
To make all five tables you will need to buy one 4-by-8-foot sheet of ¾-inch core plywood (the plywood I used is birch-faced) and two 3-foot lengths of ¼-inch dowel. If you want to cover the plywood edges, you will also need about 60 feet of paper-thin adhesive-backed veneer (known as flexible trim). A pair of ¼-inch dowel centers—small devices that make accurate doweled joints possible—is essential.

Preparing the Parts
The shapes and exact dimensions of the five tabletops and their corresponding legs are shown in Figure H. How all 25 pieces can be cut from a single 4-by-8-foot sheet of plywood is illustrated in Figure J, page 2391. There is little waste—and therefore little room for error. Follow the pattern carefully, marking the outlines of all the pieces on the plywood with a pencil and straightedge. Allow at least ⅛ inch between parts for each saw cut. Then saw out all the parts. File the edges smooth.

Rabbets and Dowels
In each table, the legs, notched to receive the top, will be held to that top with a pair of 1¼-inch-long dowels. With this construction, these delicate-looking tables will be surprisingly strong. Using the techniques described on page 2385, cut a rabbet ¾ inch deep and ½ inch wide across the inside top of each leg (Figure K, page 2391). (If you cut the rabbets a hair too deep, you can sand away the small excess later to make the joint perfect.)

When the buffet tables are nested, the legs of various shapes and sizes fit together in such a fashion that they form an almost solid cube. The five different table heights can be clearly distinguished.

This set of five buffet tables in different shapes and heights can be cut from a single 4-by-8-foot sheet of ¾-inch birch plywood, with hardly a toothpick to spare. The construction of the joints makes the tables very strong. When they are not in use, the tables nest in a compact cube (left).

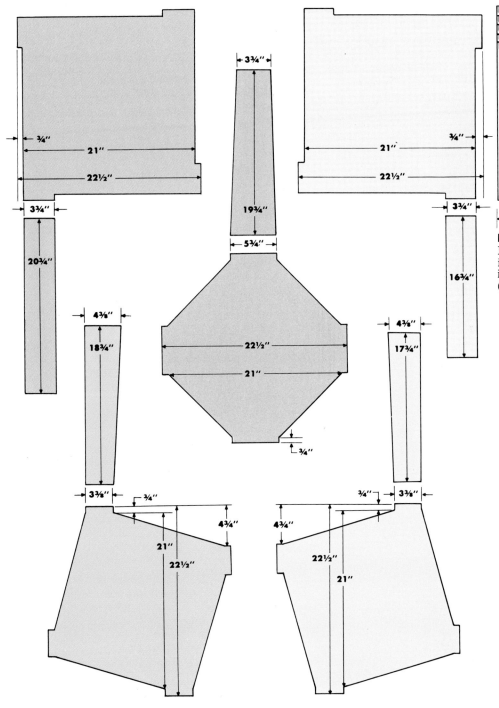

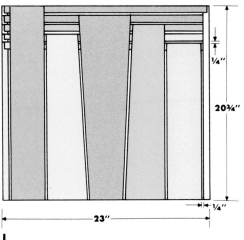

I

Figure I: The means of condensing the five nesting tables into a neat cube, as pictured opposite, is shown in this drawing, color keyed to Figure H (below left) and Figure J (page 2391).

H

Figure H: Shapes and dimensions of tops and legs for each of the five nesting tables are all different, as this drawing shows. Colors indicate which leg goes with which top and where the assembled tables fit in the nesting arrangement (Figure I). Matching colors in Figure J, page 2391, show how all the pieces needed can be cut from one standard sheet of plywood.

Dowels, glued into holes drilled in table tops and legs, help make secure joints. Cut forty 1¼-inch lengths of ¼-inch dowel. With a nail or file point, score three or four shallow grooves along the full length of each dowel. (If you like, you can buy pre-scored dowels in this standard length.) The grooves are needed to let excess glue escape from the bottom of the hole where it otherwise would be trapped by the tight-fitting dowel. Round or bevel the ends of the dowels with a knife, file, or sandpaper to make them easier to insert.

7: Test the fit of all dowel joints before you glue the legs to the tabletops. Sand two dowels until they fit slightly loosely into the holes; then use them to check all the joints in a dry run. (Full-diameter dowels would fit so tightly you couldn't remove them for gluing.)

8: To refine a joint that is one or two degrees off square at the time of gluing, raise or lower the position of the clamp heads (and the buffer scraps) until a try square fits exactly into the corner. The closer the clamp head is to the outer corner of the joint, the wider will be the angle.

Making Dowel Holes

The next step, one calling for care and patience, will be to drill holes for the dowels. These are best made with a drill press or with a hand-powered brace and bit. It is very hard to make accurately sized dowel holes with a hand-held power drill. The holes must be perpendicular, they must be the same size as the dowels, and each pair must match perfectly.

Mark centers for two holes on the bottom face of each projecting leg tab on each tabletop. Locate each one ¼ inch in from the outer edge of the tab and 1 inch in from each side edge. Wrap a piece of masking tape around a ¼-inch bit, ½ inch above the tip (this will serve as a depth gauge) and drill holes ½ inch deep at each center point. You must be careful to keep your bit at a right angle to the wood. It may help to check the accuracy of the angle with a try square, a practical tool used to lay off right angles.

To mark the center points of the matching holes to be drilled in the leg ends, use a pair of ¼-inch dowel centers; these small tools fit in the dowel holes and have pointed ends that protrude slightly. With the top upside down, position the leg as shown in Figure K and tap it lightly with a hammer (protecting it with a wood scrap). The point of each dowel center will leave an impression on the leg. Mark all the hole centers on the leg. Then place masking tape on the ¼-inch bit 1 inch from the tip, and drill two perpendicular holes to this depth in the top of each leg.

Setting the Dowels

Before gluing, test the alignment of the holes. Do not use full-diameter dowels for this purpose—they might get stuck. Instead, sand two dowels until they fit slightly loosely in the holes. Using these, test the closeness of the joint and the angle each leg makes with its top (photograph 7). Use a try square. If the two parts make a right angle without undue pressure, they are close enough to be adjusted during gluing and clamping. If not, you will need to redrill one or both pairs of dowel holes at least ¼ inch from the unsatisfactory hole or holes.

When all the holes have been tested, you are ready to glue. As shown in Figure K, the combined depth of each pair of holes is 1½ inches and each dowel is 1¼ inches long. This allows a small space for glue at each end of the dowel. Each dowel should penetrate only ⅜ inch into the tabletop and ⅞ inch into the leg. To ensure this, mark the dowels with a pencil line ⅜ inch from one end. Put all-purpose white glue in one of the tabletop holes, using a cotton swab to coat all surfaces. Immediately insert a dowel in the hole as far as the ⅜-inch mark. Gently hammer it if necessary. Continue gluing and setting the dowels in the tabletop holes, one by one. Wipe off excess glue. Let the glue dry overnight; then sand away any hardened excess that has been squeezed out, using medium-grit sandpaper.

To attach the legs to the tabletops, put glue in the holes as before and swab glue on all meeting surfaces of the joint as well. Press the dowels into their leg holes until the joint is tight. Clamp each leg, using a try square to insure an exact right angle, as described on page 2381 and shown in photograph 8.

Finishing

When the glue has dried, use medium-grit sandpaper to remove any excess wood left where the top edges of the legs adjoin the tabletops, as well as any glue that has oozed from the joints. Then smooth all surfaces lightly with fine sandpaper, sanding with the grain. Test to make sure all five tables can be stacked in a neat cube (photograph, page 2388, and Figure I, page 2389). If you wish to hide exposed edges of plywood, apply strips of self-adhesive wood veneer, available in 1-inch widths at lumberyards. Trim off any overlap with a mat knife.

The tables can be either painted or oiled. If you paint, you have your choice of high-gloss or flat enamel. I used teak oil, applied generously with a paintbrush (photograph 9). I allow it to stand for 15 or 20 minutes, then remove the excess with paper toweling (photograph 10). When you work with this oil, wear rubber or plastic gloves and avoid breathing the vapors.

For related projects and crafts, see "Antiquing Furniture," "Furniture Refinishing," "Models and Mock-ups," "Plastic Pipe Constructions," "Plywood and Foam Furnishings," "Rockers and Cradles," "Shaker Furniture," "Structural Furnishings," and "Upholstery."

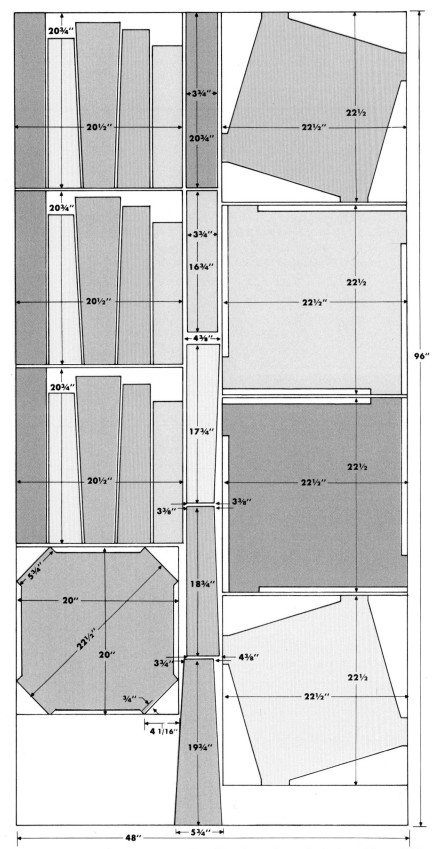

Figure J: All the table parts shown in Figures H and I can be cut from a single piece of plywood if they are carefully laid out, as shown here. Colors common to all three figures identify the parts. Allow at least ⅛ inch between parts for the saw cut. Fifteen legs can be cut from three rectangles, but the other five legs are gleaned from the center strip.

9: If you would like a simple finish that shows off the beauty of the birch veneer, brush a generous coat of teak or boiled linseed oil over all surfaces of the completed tables.

10: Let the teak oil soak into the wood for 15 or 20 minutes; then wipe away any surface excess with clean paper towels.

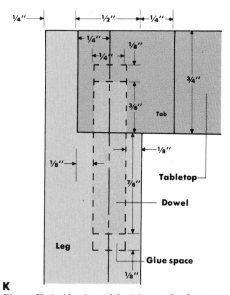

Figure K: A side view of the joint used to fasten the legs to the tabletops shows the leg notch (a rabbet) ½ inch wide and a hair more than ¾ inch deep. (The slight excess will be sanded away later.) The tabletop tab fills the rabbet (½ inch) and has an additional ¼ inch exposed. The ¼-inch dowel hole is centered in the bottom of the rabbet; it extends ½ inch into the tabletop tab and 1 inch into the leg. The 1¼-inch dowel penetrates the tab ⅜ inch and the leg ⅞ inch, leaving a ⅛-inch glue space at either end.

2391

Off-Loom Warp and Weft

When I was working at New York's Museum of Modern Art, I was assigned to prepare a catalogue for an African textiles and decorative arts exhibition. In preparation, I took a weaving course to become familiar with fibers, fabrics, and weaving techniques, including the tablet-and-frame-weaving methods that do not require a loom. I never did catalogue that exhibition—nor did I ever stop weaving.

Off-Loom Weaving

Weaving is the interlacing of a lengthwise set of threads or other material (called the warp) with a crosswise set of threads (called the weft) to form a web. To make weaving easier, the warp is often stretched on a device called a loom, so an even tension can be maintained. A loom can be as simple and nonmechanical as a twig (page 2402), or as complex as a mechanical contraption the size of a small room.

Weaving, an ancient process, began more than 20,000 years ago when early man first intertwined sticks, reeds, and rushes to make mats and baskets, without the help of a loom. Off-loom weaving is still being done—the term describes the many weaving techniques that do not require a mechanical loom. These techniques utilize the oldest, simplest, most primitive ways of creating fabric. Portability, low cost, minimum equipment, and small space requirements are attributes that have perpetuated off-loom weaving for thousands of years. For the beginner, off-loom weaving focuses attention on how various effects can be achieved with different techniques. For the experienced weaver, it provides a design freedom not possible with a mechanical loom.

Tablet and Frame Weaving

One of the oldest off-loom techniques is tablet weaving, also called card weaving (page 2394), named for the thin squares (the "tablets"—usually cardboard) used to hold the warp threads. Traces of prehistoric tablet weaving have been found in such diverse regions as Egypt, Iceland, Scandinavia, and China. The technique remains unaltered to this day. Numbered tablets function as the loom, with the warp threaded through precisely positioned holes in this loom.

An even older technique is frame weaving; the first frame probably consisted of two poles stuck in the ground. The warp is stretched over the frame, which can be a cylinder, a hoop (opposite), a wooden rectangle (page 2403), a solid geometric structure of cardboard, or a wire formation. The weaving takes its character from the shape of the frame. The frame can even become a part of the composition if the fabric is left on the frame (opposite and page 2402). The weft is woven across the warp with fingers or a needle. Since the full warp is always visible, the design can be created as the work progresses.

Sherry De Leon is a weaver who has done a great deal of experimenting with off-loom techniques, in part because she would otherwise need to find room for a mechanical loom in her small New York apartment. She has tried her hand at many crafts, designing projects for McCall's Needlework & Crafts *magazine.*

Glossary

Beating: Tightly packing the crosswise threads (weft) into position, snug against each other at one end of the lengthwise threads (warp). This can be done with fingers, a fork, or a stick beater.

Butterfly: Thread wound into a figure-eight shape to keep it from tangling as it is passed through the warp (photograph 1).

Heading: Weft woven at the beginning of a project to space the warp threads evenly and to create a foundation to beat the remaining weft against.

Pick: One passage of the weft thread through the warp threads.

Shed: The space between two layers of warp threads, through which the weft thread is passed.

Shuttle: An implement (photograph 2) on which weft thread can be wrapped for passing through the shed.

Warp: The threads that run the length of the loom, through which the weft (crosswise threads) are woven.

Weave: A particular pattern or order of interlacement for the warp and weft yarns.

Weft: The threads that run the width of the fabric; they are woven through the lengthwise threads.

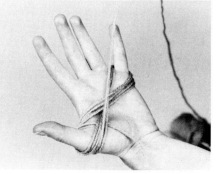

1: Yarn that will be passed back and forth can be wound into a compact bundle, called a butterfly, so it doesn't become tangled. Wrap the yarn around the thumb and little finger to form a figure-eight shape.

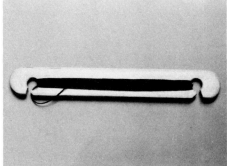

2: To ease passing the weft yarn through the warp, the yarn can be wrapped on a flat, smooth wooden paddle called a shuttle. One advantage of using a shuttle is that it can also be used as a beater to pack down the rows of weft yarn.

Sometimes the
best things in life
are free. This sunburst
made of leftover yarn was
woven to stay on the frame
as an art object, and the frame
in this case is a thick grapevine
shaped into a hoop. Directions for
weaving on a hoop are on page 2405.

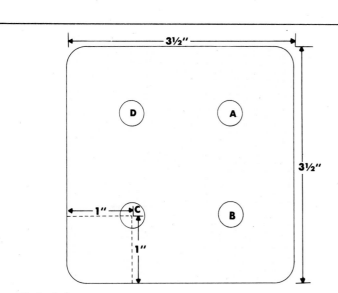

Materials

Off-loom weaving techniques require a minimum amount of equipment. For tablet weaving, you need only the tablets, plus a few household items: rubber bands; pencil; felt-tipped pen; scissors; two C-clamps; a wide-toothed comb; and a yarn needle. Tablets can be made of any thin, rigid material, but usually heavy cardboard is used. Most tablets are square with four holes and with rounded corners that facilitate turning (above), although occasionally other shapes are used. You can make your own, following the dimensions in the diagram and using a ⅜-inch paper punch to make the holes. Or you can order tablets from Lily Mills, Shelby, N. C. 28150, or Robin and Russ Handweavers, 533 North Adams St., McMinnville, Oregon 97128.

The yarns selected for the lengthwise threads (the warp) should be smooth and tightly spun. Any yarn that you can break easily with your hands is not strong enough for tablet weaving since the warp is subject to much abrasion from the constant turning of the tablets. Weaving yarn, pearl cotton, and linen work well as the warp. The crosswise threads (the weft) can be thinner than the warp threads, and usually are. The weft color should match the color of the edges of the warp, since in this type of weaving that is the only place where the weft is visible.

	1	2	3	4	5	6	7	8	9	10	11	12		
A														
B														
C														
D														

The pattern draft

The pattern draft is a shorthand way of showing how the tablets should be threaded with warp threads, indicating both the colors and arrangements of the threads.

A typical pattern draft in two colors is shown below, left. The numbers along the top of the pattern indicate how many tablets are needed; the letters along the left side match the letters assigned to the tablet holes (A, B, C, and D—marked clockwise on the face of each tablet). The two colors in this draft indicate the two colors of yarn used in the warp. Each hole in each tablet has its own warp thread; its color is indicated in the pattern draft. Arrows at the bottom of the draft indicate the direction in which the warp is threaded through the holes in the tablets. Tablets 1 through 6 are threaded front to back (indicated by arrows angling to the right); tablets 7 through 12 are threaded from back to front (indicated by arrows angling to the left).

Warping

With a pattern draft designating the number and colors of the warp threads, you are ready to measure and cut the warp yarn. But rather than measuring and cutting each thread, it is easier to wrap the entire warp at one time around two stationary objects the right distance apart. Use two C-clamps firmly attached to a table edge, a measured distance apart (above). This distance is the desired length of the finished weaving, plus almost that length again to allow for wastage, which can be used to make decorative tassels or fringe. If you were using the sample pattern draft shown, to wrap the warp for the first tablet, you would tie one end of the red thread to the left C-clamp and take it to the right C-clamp; this becomes the warp thread for hole A of tablet 1. Then take the thread around the clamp and back to the left clamp, thus measuring the warp for hole B of tablet 1. Keep the thread taut but not stretched tightly. Continue wrapping the thread around the clamps until the warp for the four holes of tablet 1 is complete.

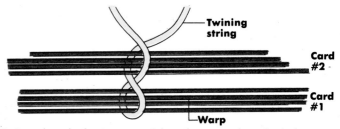

Twine a length of string around these four warp threads; do the same after wrapping the warp for each tablet to help keep the threads in order. The drawing above shows the warp for two cards being twined. You may find it helpful to make a light mark on the pattern draft so you don't lose your place. Without cutting the yarn, wrap the warp for tablet 2 as you did for tablet 1. On tablet 3, the color changes in the middle. Lay the thread of the first color aside at that point, but do not cut it off (you can pick it up again when it is needed). Tie on the new color and continue wrapping the warp.

There should not be any knots in the body of the warp. If you come to a knot, cut the thread at a clamp end, cut out the knot, and tie the ends of the thread together at the clamp before you continue wrapping. When the warping is complete, cut the threads off the C-clamps at each end, cutting through all threads.

FOR TABLET WEAVING

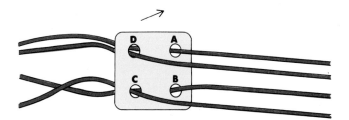

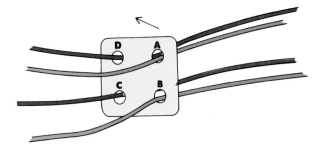

Prior to weaving, you must untangle the remaining length of warp. Slip the rubber band off the tablets. With the colored edges on top, hold the tablets loosely between spread fingers of both hands as you slide them down the warp threads toward the unknotted end. Jiggle the tablets slightly and they will slide quite easily. If the warp is too tangled for the tablets to slide freely, use your fingers or a wide-toothed comb to straighten the threads. Stretch the warp out smoothly, stopping about 10 inches from the unknotted ends. Hold the tablet pack together with the rubber band; then comb out any remaining tangles. Keeping the warp smooth and taut, tie an over-hand knot in this end of the warp as well.

First clamp   Second clamp

The newly tied end of the warp may be attached to a string or a belt around your waist, or to another C-clamp, as long as it is stretched out tightly (above).

Threading

Refer to the pattern draft to see how many tablets are needed. Then assign a number to each tablet, writing it in the space between hole D and hole A. Use a pencil so the number can be erased and the tablet reused. The tablets will be rotated as you weave. To help you keep track of their position, color the top edge of each tablet with a felt-tipped marker between D and A. You will be able to see at a glance if all of the tablets are in their original positions.

Following the pattern draft for thread color and direction (front to back or back to front), thread each warp through its designated tablet hole, bringing the warp end about 10 inches through the hole. The top drawing above shows tablet No. 1 threaded from the right, front to back, starting with hole A, with four red threads, as indicated in the draft. The second drawing above shows tablet No. 8, also threaded from the right, but back to front, starting with hole A, with two blue and two red threads, as indicated in the draft. Undo the twined string holding the weft as you thread each tablet, beginning with tablet No. 1. As each tablet is threaded, gather it with the others so all the lettered holes are in the same position and all the marked sides of the cards face the same way. Put a strong rubber band around the pack.

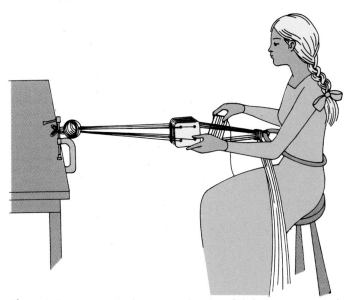

With an overhand knot (above), tie securely together the short warp ends threaded through the tablets. Using heavy string, tie the knot onto a secure object such as the C-clamp. Be sure the lettered sides of the tablets face you when the tablets are to the right of the clamp. Check the tablet threading for any mistakes; one mistake can completely throw off the pattern design.

If you tie it to your waist, be prepared to sit awhile because you need to keep the tension constant for smooth weaving. Before you begin to weave, move all the equipment you will need within easy reach.

To form a woven design, the tablets are rotated together as a single group. Each quarter-turn forms a new opening in the warp (called a shed) with the threads twisted over each other in a certain way bringing them into a new arrangement with each turn. After each turn, a crosswise thread (the weft) is passed through the shed to lock the warp threads in position, thus forming one row of the design.

These arrangements of the warp threads and the sequence in which they appear correspond to the arrangement and sequence in the pattern draft, with each horizontal row of squares in the draft representing one row of weaving.

The draft shown in the Craftnotes on pages 2394 and 2395 represents a sequence of four forward (counterclockwise) turns of the tablets, with the weaving advancing from the bottom up. These four forward turns, followed by four backward (clockwise) turns, result in the design plus its mirror image (right).

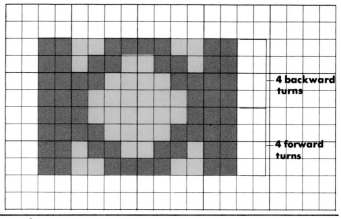

4 backward turns

4 forward turns

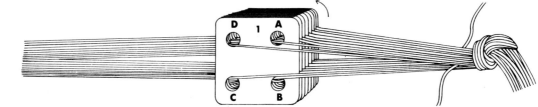

Since all the warp ends are bunched into an end knot, the first four rows of the weft are used to straighten them out. For this part of the weaving, called the heading, use a piece of heavy string as the weft. With the tablet pack still in the first position (hole A is in the upper right corner and the colored edges are all on top), insert the string weft through the shed, leaving a 4-inch end (above). Pull the string weft firmly into the angle of the warp shed.

Give the tablet pack a quarter-turn forward into the second position, bringing hole B to the upper right corner. Use the string to make a second weft pick, going through the new shed in the direction opposite to the first (above).

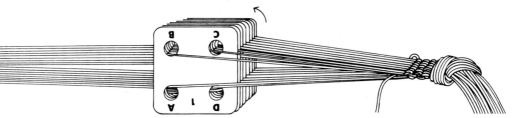

Make a second quarter-turn of the tablet pack, moving hole C into the upper right corner, then take a third weft pick (above).

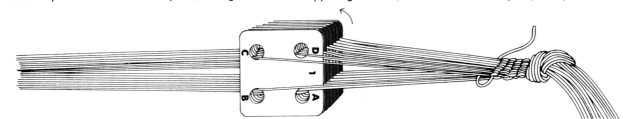

Make a third quarter-turn of the tablet pack, moving hole D into the upper right corner, then take a fourth weft pick (above).

WEAVING ON TABLETS

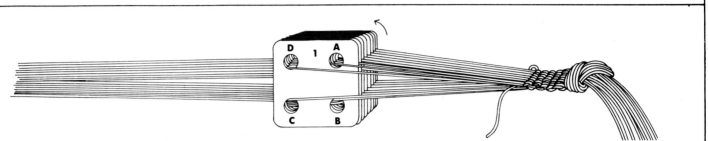

Make the fourth quarter-turn of the tablet pack to return the tablets to their original position, with the colored edges on top (above). The warp is now evenly spaced so you are ready to begin weaving. Leave the ends of string; the heading will be removed when the weaving is completed. To make turning the tablets easier, hold them loosely between the spread fingers of both hands; if necessary, jiggle them slightly.

Wind a length of weft thread into a butterfly or onto a wooden or cardboard shuttle (photographs 1 and 2, page 2392). There is a knack to throwing the weft that you will acquire, so the warp threads are not bunched up nor the weft thread loop protruding at the sides. With practice, you will be able to judge the proper tension. Try placing the weft in the shed firmly against the existing weaving, while letting the loop show at the edge; then gently pull on the weft until the slack is taken up in the loop. But do not pull so hard the warp bunches up. After each turn of the tablets, clear the shed before you take that weft pick, as this helps keep the design distinct. To do this, use the edge of the shuttle or a comb to force the last warp thread tightly against the adjacent warp thread. This process is called beating down; the result is that the shed is cleared. Sliding the tablet pack down the warp against the weaving, then sliding it away, will also clear the shed.

Begin weaving with the tablets in their original position; clear the shed. Leaving a 4-inch end of weft free, take a weft pick. Then turn the tablet pack one quarter-turn forward into the second position (just as you did to weave in the string weft). Continue turning the

tablets and passing the weft through the shed each time, until the tablets are back in the original position. Four forward quarter-turns and four backward quarter-turns complete one pattern repeat. Continue turning the tablets in the same sequence throughout the weaving process.

Note that as the tablets turn, the warp threads twist and untwist. In order to keep the edges as tight and smooth as possible, turn the two outer tablets on each side in the same direction for as long as possible; when those threads become very twisted, reverse their direction for awhile. Therefore, in making the second four quarter-turns, which are backward, keep turning the two outer tablets on each edge forward. Since these tablets carry a single color of yarn, the design will not be affected. Turn the tablets in their respective directions, then pass the weft pick through the shed in the same manner as you previously did. The outer edge tablets will follow the positions of the first four turns; the inner pack will have a new position, first with D in the upper right corner, then C, then B.

If you must interrupt your weaving, stop when the tablets are in the original position with the marked edges on top. Pull them up against the weaving, then tie the pack together or hold it with a rubber band. If the woven pattern is not distinct, you have made a mistake in threading or turning; check both. If you notice a mistake several turns after it was made, turn the tablets in the reverse direction and remove the weft after each turn until you eliminate the error. Mistakes come out easily with pearl cotton or linen, less easily with fuzzy wools.

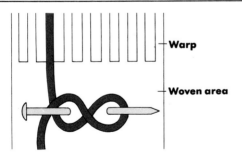

- Warp
- Woven area

Broken Warp

If a warp thread breaks, cut a new one of the original length. Tie one end onto the far C-clamp, bring the thread through the proper hole in its tablet, and pin the free end onto the woven area in a figure eight (above). When the weaving is completed, use a needle to weave in both broken and pinned ends, following the direction of the warp threads.

When you need a new weft thread, take a pick with the old weft thread, leaving a 6-inch end hanging free. Then take the same pick

in the opposite direction with the new weft, again letting a 6-inch end hang free. Turn the tablets and take the next pick with the end of the old weft and the new weft, in opposite directions. Turn the tablets and continue with the new weft, cutting off the old weft close to the edge. Finally, weave the free end of the new weft across and cut it off close to the edge.

As the weaving progresses, you may find it awkward to reach comfortably if the weaving is tied to your waist. In that case, undo the tie or belt at your waist. Tie the woven part of the strip in a knot; then tie that knot to your waist.

When you approach the end, the unwoven warp thread will be very twisted. To get maximum yardage, untie the knot at the clamp, being sure to follow the procedure for interrupting the weaving process that was described earlier. Undo the knot of warp ends and comb out the tangles. Retie the knot and reanchor the warp to the clamp. Continue weaving until there is no longer enough warp space to turn the tablets. Stop weaving at the end of a pattern repeat. Using a yarn needle, weave the end of the weft thread back into the last few rows of weaving. At the beginning of the weaving, weave in the first weft end the same way.

Finishing

Untie the ends from the anchor points and remove the warp knots. Carefully unthread the tablets and remove the heading at the beginning. Finish the ends with a plain, wrapped, or twisted fringe, as described in the project directions that follow.

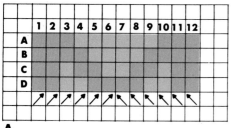

A

Figure A: As described in the Craftnotes (pages 2394 and 2395), follow this drafting pattern when you thread the tablets for weaving the belt shown at right.

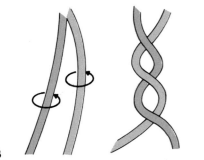

B

Figure B: To make a twisted cord, as shown at the ends of the belt, right, work with the warp ends from two adjacent tablets at a time. Anchor the woven belt on a table with a heavy weight such as a book, or tie it around a door knob to keep it stationary. Holding a group of four threads between the thumb and first two fingers of each hand, twist each group to the right (shown at left). When the threads are well twisted and begin to kink, twist them together toward your right (shown at right). When the twisted portion is the right length, tie the ends together with an overhand knot to keep them from untwisting.

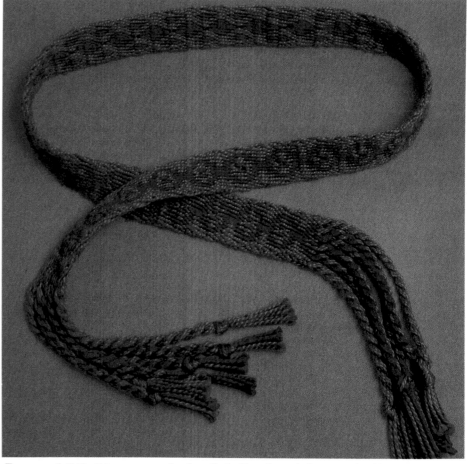

To weave a belt like this, you use cards, also called tablets, instead of a conventional loom. This type of weaving produces this thick, flat, narrow band with a different design on each side.

Weaving, Braiding, and Knotting
Tablet-woven belt

The two-color belt pictured above is meant to be fastened at the waist by tying one twisted cord from one belt end to a twisted cord on the opposite belt end.

Materials
To make the belt in the colors and yarn shown, you will need No. 5 pearl cotton in royal blue and kelly green. The amount will vary according to your waist measurement; approximately 50 yards of green and 28 yards of blue will make a 28- to 30-inch belt with 4-inch-long tassels at either end. You will also need the materials listed in the Craftnotes on page 2394.

Weaving
Take your waist measurement over garments and add 2 feet to that for the basic warp length. Directions for card weaving are given in the Craftnotes, pages 2394 through 2397. Following the pattern draft in Figure A, cut the warp and thread the cards. Follow the four-turns-forward and four-turns-backward weaving sequence to weave the belt. Weave until you have completed your waist measurement. (Be sure not to count the heading at the beginning.)

Finishing
Weave in the weft ends, remove the C-clamps, untie the overhand knots, and remove the heading as described in the Craftnotes (page 2397). To finish the warp ends, make six twisted cords at each end of the belt as shown in Figure B. Trim the ends about 1 inch beyond each knot.

This shoulder bag was made from two strips woven with tablets. The same weaving pattern was used for both strips, but the colors were changed. The strips were sewn together to form the pocket, and a twisted cord was added for a shoulder strap.

Weaving, Braiding, and Knotting
Bag of tablet-woven strips

The bag pictured above is made by joining two long woven strips. The warp ends are wrapped to form the tassel trim on the flap, and a twisted cord is added to serve as the strap.

Materials
In addition to the materials listed in the Craftnotes (page 2394), you will need No. 5 pearl cotton in these amounts (1 yard for leeway has been added to each): for strip one—blue, 33 yards, plus 17 yards for weft and finishing; light green, 57 yards; kelly green, 73 yards; and orange, 33 yards; for strip two—kelly green, 33 yards, plus 17 yards for weft and finishing; pink, 57 yards; orange, 29 yards; rust, 33 yards; and light green, 45 yards. For the twisted cord you will need 12 yards each of light green, rust, orange, and pink.

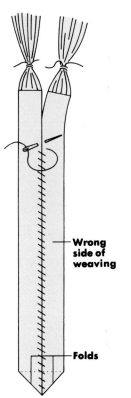

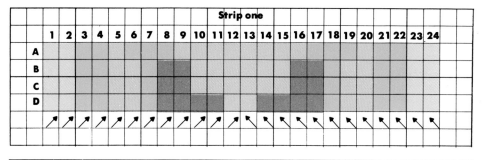

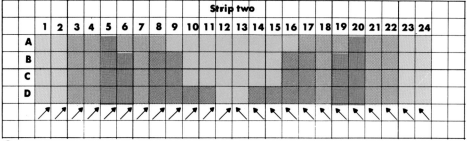

Figure C: Follow these pattern drafts when you thread the tablets to make the strips for the shoulder bag (Craftnotes, pages 2394 and 2395).

D

Figure D: Fold each woven strip in half, forming a point. Try to match the pattern motifs on each side. With weft thread, slip-stitch the two inner edges together, from the pointed fold to the ends.

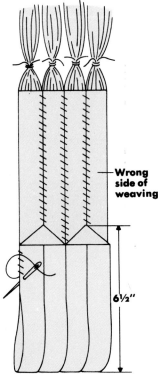

E

Figure E: Wrong sides together, fold up the pointed ends of the bag 6½ inches. Using matching thread, slip-stitch the sides from the base of the points to the bottom fold.

Weaving

The basic procedures for tablet weaving are given in the Craftnotes on pages 2394 through 2397. Each of the two strips needed in this project is made separately, using the same design but different colors. Follow the pattern drafts in Figure C when you count and measure the warp and when you thread the tablets for strip one and strip two. All warp threads are 2 yards long; the finished length of each woven strip is 40 inches long, not counting the tassels. Measure the warp, thread the tablets, and weave one strip at a time. Weave using the four-forward, four-backward sequence. When you have completed 40 inches of weaving, use a needle to weave the weft ends into the weaving. Then undo the overhand knots, and remove the tablets and the heading. Temporarily tie a length of string around the loose warp ends of each strip.

Assembling the Bag

Fold each strip as shown in Figure D and sew their inner edges together on the wrong side of the weaving. Place the two folded-and-sewn strips side by side with pointed ends and loose ends equal; slipstitch them together where they meet. Then fold the pointed ends up, and use matching thread to stitch the sides together, forming a pocket (Figure E). Remove the temporary string ties and wrap the warp ends, forming tassels (Figure F).

To make the twisted cord for the strap, cut six 2-yard strands each of light green, rust, orange, and pink. Tie the strands together at one end with a single large over-

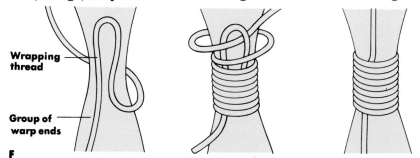

F

Figure F: To finish the warp ends of strips used in the bag, use weft thread to wrap the ends in groups, close to the end of the weaving. Form a loop of weft thread; lay it on top of, and parallel to, the warp ends (left). Then wrap the thread around the loop and the warp ends for about 1 inch. Using a needle, insert the end of the wrapping thread through the loop (center). Then pull the loop end and the wrapping thread end in opposite directions until the loop is pulled underneath the wrapping (right). Trim the ends as close to the wrapping as possible.

hand knot. Anchor the knotted end by placing it under a heavy object or catching it in a drawer. Divide the strands into two groups, with three strands of each color in each group. Twist both groups of strands to the left until they begin to kink. Then twist both groups together to the right (Figure B, page 2398). When the strands are well twisted, tie the free ends together with another overhand knot. Trim the ends close to the knots. Overlap the two knotted ends and conceal them by wrapping (Figure F), thus forming one continuous twisted cord.

With the joined area of the strap under the flap of the bag, stitch the cord to the inside of the fold in the flap.

CRAFTNOTES: FRAME WEAVING

To do frame weaving, you can use any sturdy frame. It can be made with artist's canvas stretchers, a recycled picture frame, a tree branch, or even a grapevine hoop. After you try a frame weaving or two, other possibilities will occur to you.

For frame weaving, use a sturdy yarn for the lengthwise threads (warp) such as a wool rug yarn, a good cotton yarn, or strong string. Any yarn can be used for the crosswise threads (weft), since they receive little stress.

Warping
Once the frame has been selected, the first step is warping it. The warp is stretched on the frame tight enough so the threads will stay in place but not so tight that great strain is put on either the warp threads or the frame. The way in which the warp is stretched on the frame varies according to the type of frame used (see project directions).

Weaving
The space between the two layers of warp threads form one shed. For the countershed, the warp threads from the lower layer must be lifted up with thumb and forefinger and raised higher than the top layer of warp before you pass the weft thread through.

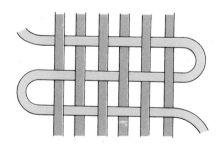

The most basic weave is called plain weave. The weft moves alternately over and under adjacent warps. This sequence is reversed in each alternate weft (above).

If the yarns are similar in weight, this produces fabric that exposes half warp and half weft. In the case of tapestry weaving, where a soft, pliable yarn weft is used with a thin, taut string warp, the weft can be made to hide the warp, producing a weft-faced fabric. There are also warp-faced fabrics (such as those produced by tablet weaving, pages 2398 and 2399) where only the warp is visible.

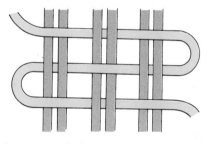

A variation of plain weave is the rep weave. The rep weave is made by extending the plain weave either vertically or horizontally. In a weft-faced rep (above) the weft goes over and under two or more warp yarns at a time.

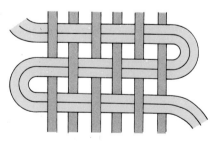

In a warp-faced rep (above), the weft yarn is double or more as it goes over and under one warp thread at a time.

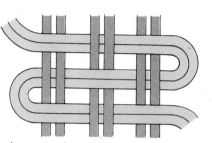

Basket weave has two or more weft yarns interlaced with two or more warp yarns (above). For both the weft-faced rep and basket weaves, both the shed and countershed must be lifted so you can weave over and under two warps at a time.

To prepare your weft, wrap the yarns into butterflies (photograph 1, page 2392). As you weave, force down each pick (the inserted weft) after it is taken. When the weft turns the corner going from one pick to another, do not pull tightly on the threads—this will cause the fabric to pull in. If you find this is happening, try leaving a small loop at the edge. With practice, the feel of the right weft tension will come to you. If you run out of weft thread or wish to change colors, leave a 2-inch weft end on the underside of the weaving. Begin with a new weft where the old weft stopped, leaving a 2-inch end on the underside. If you think the ends might come undone or the weave is so open they are visible from the front, use a yarn needle to weave these ends into the previous weaving.

A lively totem resulted when natural yarns such as unspun wool and raffia were woven on a Y-shaped tree branch.

Looms do grow on trees; Gaea, a beginning weaver, is learning the art on a Y-shaped branch, a loom that can be found almost anywhere.

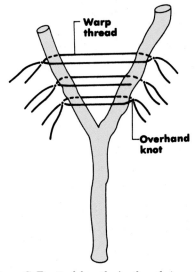

G

Figure G: To attach lengthwise threads (warp) to a Y-shaped branch for weaving, tie them on in pairs, using an overhand knot at either end.

Weaving on a branch

For your weaving frame, cut a Y-shaped tree branch that is still a bit green—a dry one would be too brittle and might break. For the lengthwise threads (warp), use a strong yarn—the weaving pictured above, left, required about 35 yards of rug yarn. For the crosswise threads (weft), use small amounts of various fibers such as unspun wool, raffia, and other natural yarns.

Weaving
Cut the warp yarn into pairs of threads that will fit across the Y branch at ½-inch intervals. Allow an extra 8 inches at each end for knots and fringes. About 8 inches from one end, tie an overhand knot in each pair of warp threads. Beginning at the narrowest point of the Y, place this knot on the outside of one branch. Then stretch the two warp threads across to the outside of the opposite branch, and tie another overhand knot (Figure G). Continue warping at about ½-inch intervals, depending on the branch.

When the warping is complete, you are ready to weave. To weave, hold the branch with the warp threads vertical. Use the plain, rep, and basket weaves as described in the Craftnotes, page 2401). Use a separately cut weft thread for each one or two picks, leaving long ends to hang as a decorative fringe. Weave some areas tightly to contrast with unwoven areas. Display the different textures of the yarns, and combine fibers and change colors as you wish. (It is easier to use the lighter-weight fibers at the narrow end and the heavier ones at the open end.)

Using only two colors of yarn, this geometric design was woven on a rectangular wooden frame, with the simplest of weaving techniques.

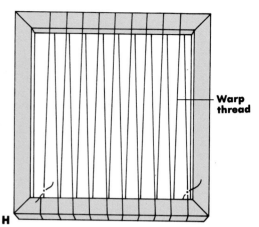

H

Figure H: To warp a rectangular frame loom (that is, to wrap on the stationary lengthwise threads), knot the warp thread onto the bottom strip at the left corner, catching the thread in the first edge notch. Then start winding by taking the thread to the top and over the front of the top strip (catching the first notch at the top). Then take it to the back, down, over the front of the bottom strip (to the second bottom notch), and around to the back, so you create a figure eight of thread. Continue winding, catching the thread in succeeding notches, until you have a total of 100 such warp threads. The drawing shows only a few warp threads for clarity.

Weaving, Braiding, and Knotting
Geometric frame weaving

Artist's canvas stretchers, available at art supply stores, were used to make the weaving pictured above. Any kind of wood strips that can be joined at right angles to make a square or rectangle will serve as a frame loom—even a sturdy old picture frame. Just be sure the loom is strong enough to withstand the tension of the warp and that its corners are square.

Materials
To make the 9-by-10-inch weaving, you will need 9-by-16-inch paper; four 16-inch artist's canvas stretchers; glue or small screws; a screwdriver; ruler; pencil; handsaw; sandpaper; scissors or single-edged razor blade; yarn needle; about 47 yards of tightly spun smooth yarn (for the warp); 2 ounces each of two yarns in contrasting colors, one the same color as the warp and both the same weight as the warp (for the weft). I used green rug wool for the warp, and green and purple rug wool for the weft. To beat down each weft thread, use a table fork.

Making and Warping the Loom
If you are using wood stretchers to make the frame loom, fit them together, making sure the corners are square. Glue or screw each corner to maintain the shape of the frame while you weave. Measure in from each corner on the top and bottom edges of the frame so you leave a centered 10-inch area between marks as the warp area. Use pencil and ruler to divide this warp area into inches. Then divide each inch into fifths (this can be approximate), making a total of 50 marks. Lightly draw a saw blade across each mark to make a series of shallow notches in the wood. After sawing, sand the wood enough to clear away any splinters.

To warp the frame, tie the end of the warp yarn around the bottom stretcher bar with the yarn in the first notch. The warping motion makes a figure eight around the frame (Figure H). As you wind, keep the yarn tight enough so it does not sag, but do not stretch it.

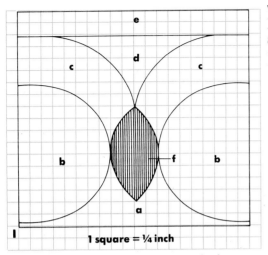

Figure I: To make a full-sized pattern for the geometric weaving pictured on page 2403, enlarge this design by copying it square by square on paper that you have ruled in ¼-inch squares. Pin the pattern to the back of the warp threads so you can follow the outlines and the weave-and-color key below.

Weave-and-color key

a: green (plain weave)
b: purple (warp-faced rep weave with two weft threads)
c: green (plain weave)
d: purple (weft-faced rep weave over two warp threads)
e: purple (plain weave)
f: purple (wrapped over 11 pairs of warp threads)

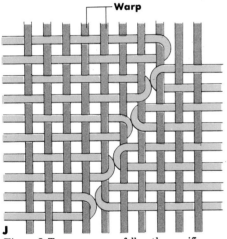

Figure J: To weave as you follow the specific shapes of a pattern, weave back and forth with the designated color of yarn, reversing it when you come to the edge of the outlined area. But work with whatever colors of weft thread are needed so you can complete one full row at a time.

Weaving

Enlarge the pattern for the design (Figure I), and darken the lines. Center this full-sized pattern under the frame and tape or pin it to the warp. The darkened outlines of the design will show through the warp and you will be able to follow them as you weave. Wrap the weft yarns into several butterflies (photograph 1, page 2392.)

Begin by weaving several rows of plain weave, (for weaving techniques, see Craftnotes, page 2401), with green yarn at the edge closest to you (bottom of the design). For the first row, lift up the lower layer of warp threads and take a green weft pick across the full width of the warp. Leave a 4-inch tail of the weft yarn free. Beat the weft down with a fork. Before weaving row two, tuck the free 4-inch weft tail through the shed (the space between the warp threads) as if weaving the second row. With the weft, turn the corner at the side edge and take a second weft pick across the full warp. Weave a few more rows of green plain weave.

Continue weaving. Follow the pattern under the warp and the key (Figure 1). To follow a shaped area of the design, work entirely across each pick. Use butterflies of different colors as necessary. As you take the pick, weave the required color in that outlined area only. At the edge of the area, leave the butterfly dangling in place. Beat down as you complete each pick. Take the next pick in the opposite direction. Reverse the yarn within the square as necessary (Figure J). Continue weaving back and forth in the outlined areas, with the weft yarns of adjacent areas lying next to each other between the warp threads. Divide the 22 threads in pairs and wrap each pair. For shorter wrapped lengths, use the technique described in Figure F. For longer lengths, fold the ends along the warp; wrap to cover the ends and secure. Wrap the specified distance. Use a yarn needle to thread the end under the wrapping. Clip end close to wrapping.

When the weaving is complete, use scissors or a razor blade to cut the warp threads off the frame, cutting the warp in the center of the outer edges of the stretcher strips so the ends will be equal. At both ends, tie each adjacent pair of warp threads in an overhand knot up close to the weaving.

Weaving, Braiding, and Knotting
Landscape frame weaving $ ⧗ 👥 🎨

The small landscape scene pictured opposite was woven on the same loom as the geometric frame weaving (page 2403). For the warp yarn, you will need 47 yards of a strong, heavy yarn. (I used camel-colored rug wool.) For the weft, you will need small amounts of various types of yarn in several colors. (I used blue, purple, green, brown, orange, yellow, and red.) To finish the hanging, you will need two ¼-inch wooden dowels, 12 inches long. Warp the loom following the directions given for the geometric weaving (Figure H).

To weave, refer to the color photograph and to the directions in the Craftnotes, page 2401. For some tightly woven areas, it will help if you thread lengths of weft yarn onto a yarn needle; use the point of the needle to lift up the warp yarn.

Begin by weaving several rows of plain weave with blue yarn. With purple yarn, weave several picks of warp-faced rep weave (see Craftnotes, page 2401), decreasing the pick length from across the full warp to across about 1½ inches in the middle. Using a *soumak* weave (Figure K) weave a series of curved rows, representing hills, in green and brown yarn. In the valley made by the hills on the left side, weave an orange sun of basket weave. Give the sun a halo of yellow, red, and orange picks of plain weave that curve around it. In the same color yarns, use plain weave, wrapping (Figure F, page 2400), and *soumak* to make random sun rays. To make the hint of blue sky, use blue yarn in plain weave and warp-faced rep weave to weave three curving sections.

Cut the weaving off the frame as for the geometric weaving. Just below the blue at the lower edge, insert one of the dowels in the warp shed. Knot pairs of adjacent warp ends together over the dowel with square knots (Figure L). At the top edge, about 2 inches down, tie adjacent pairs of warp threads together in an overhand knot. Insert another dowel between pairs of threads above the knots. Using an overhand knot, tie pairs of threads around the dowel.

This sunny landscape was woven with small amounts of brightly colored yarn on the same wooden frame used to weave the geometric design on page 2403.

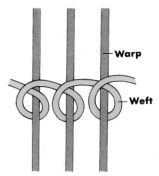

K

Figure K: The *soumak* weave, used to make woven lines, is actually a wrapping technique, since the crosswise thread (weft) encircles each lengthwise thread (warp). Pass the weft thread over the warp thread, looping behind it and then over itself in front.

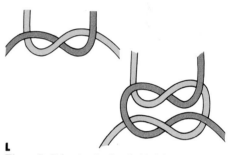

L

Figure L: To make the first half of the square knot, bring the right cord over the left cord; then loop the left cord over and under the right cord (top). Tighten the first half of the knot. Bring what is now the left cord over the right one; loop the right cord over and under the left cord (bottom). Tighten the completed knot.

Weaving, Braiding, and Knotting

Hoop weaving

$ ⊠ 👫 🐑

For the weaving pictured on page 2393 you need a hoop about 12 inches in diameter, such as a large embroidery hoop. I used a thick green grapevine that I curved and tied into a circle, then let dry. For the warp you will need about 44 yards of a strong wool; I used mostly orange rug wool with a bit of red rug wool. For weft, use several yellow yarns in varying weights and textures.

The warping of the hoop is done in a figure-8 motion (Figure M). Continue wrapping the warp over the hoop, always going from front to back around the frame, and crossing in the middle. Space warp threads randomly ¼ to ½ inch apart, and skip some 2- to 3-inch areas on the hoop entirely. When the warping is completed, tie the end onto the hoop.

Wind weft yarns into butterflies (photograph 1, page 2392). Referring to the Craftnotes on page 2401, begin weaving in the center, using a plain weave with rows that form a circle. Work several rows around, beating the weft into the center of the warp. Then work in several random warp areas (groups of 8 to 10 warp threads). Weave back and forth in plain, rep, or basket weaves. Repeat several circles of plain weave. Then weave again on groups of warp threads. As you near the hoop, pull tightly on the warp threads to make the weaving form a point. On pairs of warp threads, wrap from the woven area up to the hoop (Figure F, page 2400). Leave some unwoven warp threads. Do not cut the weaving from the hoop; the hoop is an integral part of the design.

For related entries, see "Inkle Weaving," "Rya and Flossa," "Weaving," and "Woven Tapestries."

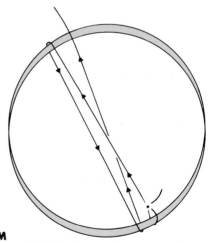

M

Figure M: To begin wrapping warp thread around a hoop, tie one end of it onto the hoop. Then take the yarn across the center of the hoop to the other side, directly opposite the knot. Carry the warp from the front of the hoop around to the back; then bring it back across the center. Place this wrap ¼ to ½ inch away from the knot, bringing the yarn across the front of the hoop around to the back. Continue wrapping, making figure eights and crossing the center each time, until the warp yarn is used up.

TAMBOUR
A Hooked Embroidery

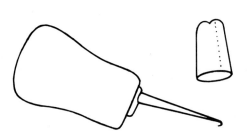

Bernice Barsky of New York designs handwork for magazines and needlecraft manufacturers, and translates French and Italian handwork instructions. She prepared tambour design samples for yardage to be executed in India and four pre-Columbian designs for the Metropolitan Museum of Art gift shop in New York. She has been a mechanical draftsman, technical editor, owner of a hand-knitting shop, and designer of knitted textiles.

If you love to do handwork, but have only limited time for it, tambour—a hooked embroidery—may be the craft for you. The technique is a simple one, essentially that of making a crocheted chain. The big difference is that the tambour chain is worked on a base fabric. This fabric—an open weave is best—is stretched over a frame. A tambour hook, or a crochet hook with a pointed tip, is inserted through the taut fabric, catches yarn or thread held under the fabric, then draws that yarn up to the surface as a loop on the hook. Retaining that loop, the hook again pierces the fabric a short distance away and catches the yarn to bring another loop to the surface. The second loop is then drawn through the first. As this is repeated over and over again, a chained line is formed on the face of the fabric, which seems better shaped than needle-made stitches and is more quickly worked. The joy of the tambour technique is that with practice, your movements will develop a flowing rhythm and speed.

From East to West

The origins of tambour are not known, but experts believe its forerunner originated in India. There, an *ārī*, a small hook similar to the tambour hook (lower left), was used to embroider gold and silver threads onto leather. At the start of the sixteenth century, Europeans learned of these beautiful embroideries, so finely stitched and so subtly colored that it was difficult to distinguish them from paintings. The fashion interest in Indian crewelwork had begun. How the *ārī* became the tambour hook is not known. Nor do we know when the tambourinelike frame that gave the craft its name was introduced. But by the mid-1800s, tambour was established in many parts of Europe. Shortly thereafter, it made its way to America.

Different cultures made different uses of tambour. This craft involves only one basic stitch, but the choice of thread and fabric produces a variety of effects. In

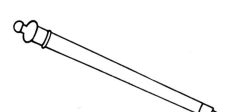

A

Figure A: Above are the Victorian tambour hook and thimble (top) and the *ārī* (at bottom), an Indian embroidery tool from which the tambour hook is derived. The tambour hook had a handle that could accommodate hooks of various sizes. The brass thimble, open at the top and notched on the sides, did more than protect dainty fingers; it provided a guide for the hook to slide on.

Professional Indian embroiderers have used the *ārī* for centuries to produce colorful chain-stitch designs. Reproduced above is a nineteenth-century painting that depicts Khaliq embroiderers at work, holding the *ārī* and the thread, with the fabric draped over one arm in the traditional position.

Opposite: These tambour details, done in the *Tree of Life* style, are representative of contemporary chain embroidery from India. These crewelwork pieces were embroidered with the *ārī* (Figure A).

Left to right, above: Three progressively larger details of an antique Turkish coverlet show the fluid lines that can be achieved by chain stitching with a hook. These stitches were made with metallic thread that is now tarnished. Imagine how spectacular this coverlet must have been when it was new.

Switzerland and Germany, white work, done with white yarn on white fabric, was treasured. Many young women earned their living hooking white thread through translucent muslin or cambric to ornament dresses, caps, and curtains. Delicate embroideries were highly regarded in Ireland, too; there, luxurious floral designs were worked on net. These came to be known as Limerick lace. In America, where strong, colorful ornamentation was often favored, tambour work resulted in such masterpieces as the Caswell carpet, one of the most famous of American folk embroideries. Now in the Metropolitan Museum of Art in New York, the carpet was made in the mid-1800s by a young, untutored Vermont girl, Zeruah Highsley Guernsey, who later became Zeruah Caswell. The carpet has inspired many needlework designs, understandable since it contains 66 separate motifs in its 12 by 13½ feet. Most are floral patterns; one of the most beautiful of these, reminiscent of Indian crewelwork, inspired the leafy pillow (page 2416). Only three squares in the Caswell carpet are not worked on a solid-color background; two of these depict cats. One of the cats is a startling bright blue, a departure from the realistic coloring of the rest of the carpet and one of the most interesting motifs for that reason. Mrs. Caswell's blue cat was the inspiration for the wall hanging on page 2415.

Modern Adaptations

Almost anything that can be decorated with embroidery can be tamboured, providing the hook and yarn used will easily pass through the fabric. Clothing, curtains, pillows, and carpets can be decorated and wall hangings made, as projects that follow illustrate. Tambour work need not be limited to one technique, either; it can be combined with quilting, appliqué, sewing, and other needlecrafts, as in the dragonfly medallion on page 2418.

To get started with tambour work, you need: an open-weave fabric; embroidery thread or yarn; a tambour or crochet hook; scissors; and a frame or embroidery hoop. These materials are described in detail opposite. The Craftnotes on pages 2410 and 2411 show how to make the chain stitch and how to block the finished tambour work.

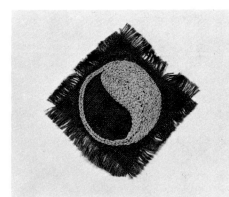

1: This practice piece of tambour work was made with ordinary string worked on a square of burlap (see Craftnotes, page 2410.)

On Practice

Tambour can be used for quick results, but practice is necessary if you are to do it well. None of these projects should be attempted until you have become familiar with the chain stitch technique. Using inexpensive fabric and yarn, practice the stitch without a prearranged pattern. Since curved lines are easier to make than straight lines; try those first. Experiment until you can make smooth, evenly spaced stitches on the fabric every time. As you become familiar with the technique, you will find that you must adjust the loop less and less often to obtain uniform stitches.

Two practice pieces are shown at left. Make several like these. You will soon be able to tambour easily and rapidly. You can work in any direction without changing the position of your frame by simply bringing the yarn over the hook from the opposite side when you want to change directions. Once you master the chain stitch, other techniques described here will come easily. But do a beginner's project or two before you attempt a complicated one such as the dragonfly medallion.

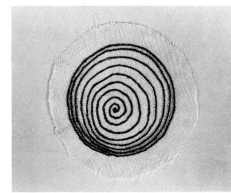

2: Cotton net was used as the background fabric for tambouring this practice swirl that includes two weights of pearl cotton.

CRAFTNOTES: TOOLS AND MATERIALS

The basic tools and materials used in tambour work are: a hook; scissors; the background fabric; thread or yarn; a crochet or rug hook; and a hoop or frame.

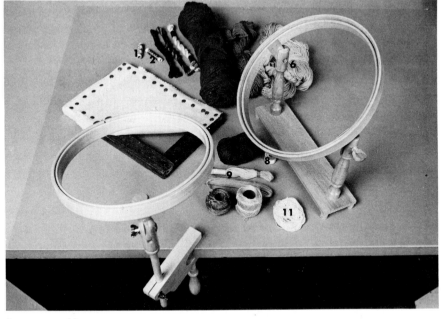

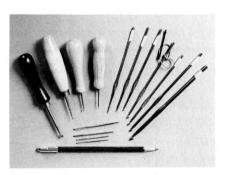

The size of the hook you need depends on the size of the openings between the threads of your fabric and the thickness of the yarn. Small hooks and thin yarn are used with tightly woven fabrics and larger hooks and thicker yarn with loosely woven fabrics. I attach a bobby pin to the handle of my hook with a rubber band (fourth crochet hook from the right) to anchor the chain-stitch loop when my work is interrupted.

Tapestry needles (center) are used to weave thread ends into the wrong side of the tambour to create an endless chain. At the bottom of the picture is a transfer pencil for transferring a design to fabric.

Frames and hoops

For tambour, the fabric being worked must be stretched; three devices for doing this are pictured above. Artist's canvas stretchers (center left) or large embroidery hoops (bottom left and right) will keep the fabric taut while you work. I prefer a frame because the fabric is less distorted than when a hoop is used. But with delicate fabrics that might be marred by tacks or for designs that have floating motifs which can be worked as separate units, I use a hoop. Either the type supported by legs or one which can be screwed to the edge of a table will keep both hands free for tambouring. The top hoop should also be adjustable for different thicknesses of fabric. Hoops like these are available at needlework shops. If you use a canvas-stretcher frame, available in many sizes at art-supply stores, prop it up on coffee cans or books, so one hand can move freely under it. Use rustproof tacks to attach the fabric to the frame. If the frame is smaller than the fabric, you can untack and move the fabric as you complete an area. Usually any marring of the fabric can be corrected during the blocking process (page 2411). If you must insert tacks in a previously tamboured area, use pushpins with a ½- to ⅝-inch pin, and put a layer of tissue paper between the work and the pin. To secure the fabric in a hoop, lay it on the bottom ring; place the top ring over it and press down, being sure the grain of the fabric is not pulled on a bias. You can tape or sew tissue paper or velvet to the bottom ring, as shown on page 2412, to cushion delicate fabrics. Avoid leaving fabric in a hoop overnight; it might become permanently pressure-marked.

Threads and yarns

In general, use firmly spun and twisted threads and yarns for tambour work. These are less likely to split than softer yarns. Relate the thread to the fabric; it should be coarser than the fabric threads (to give an illusion of depth), but thin enough to be passed easily through the fabric. I work directly from a spool or ball of yarn, because a free running thread is best for tambour, and joinings can be kept to a minimum. A variety of threads and yarns well suited to tambour is pictured above: metallic thread (1), buttonhole twist (2) and (8), pearl cotton (3) and (10), rug wool (4), rya wool (5), crochet cotton (6), linen (7), and embroidery wool (9). Many other materials can be used, even string (11).

Hooks and needles

To pull the yarn through the fabric, you will need a tambour or crochet hook. You may be lucky enough to find a real tambour hook or even an Indian ārī, though neither is readily available. If not, crochet hooks (the seven at the right, top right photograph) or rug hooks (the four at the left with handles) can be used. Choose a hook with a pointed tip, rather than a rounded one, so it will penetrate the fabric more easily.

Fabrics

Any strong, open-weave fabric can be used as the background material for tambour. It is important that the hook penetrate the fabric easily and pull up the tambour yarn without catching or breaking fabric threads. Test a small swatch before starting a project. If the surface is to be entirely covered (as in the wool rug, page 2413), these are the only requirements, but if only part of the fabric will be covered, the color and texture of the background material become important. For items that will be laundered, preshrink the fabric. Bind the edges of loosely woven material with hand- or machine-stitching.

In the selection of possible fabrics pictured above from left to right are: cotton net, theatrical gauze, monk's cloth with woven guidelines, marquisette, burlap, and hardanger cloth.

You are ready to begin tambouring when your design has been transferred onto the background fabric (opposite page) and the fabric has been mounted on a hoop or canvas stretcher.

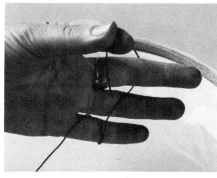

To start the chain stitch
Hold the thread in your left hand, as pictured above, or handle it the way you would if you were crocheting. (Note: If you are left-handed, use a mirror to follow these photographs.)

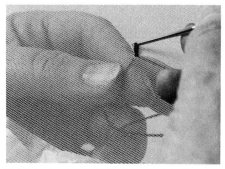

Hold the hook vertically in your right hand above the frame; with your left hand hold the thread under the frame. Insert the hook through the fabric at the starting point of your design, catch the thread, and pull a loop up through the fabric with the hook (above).

Keeping this loop loosely on the shaft of the hook, push the hook through the fabric a short distance away and pull up another loop; the exact distance is determined by how long you want the stitches to be.

Draw the second loop through the first, forming the first chain stitch. Continue to make new loops in this way, drawing each through the previous one, as pictured. Keep the loop on the hook shaft loose, but maintain only enough tension on the bottom thread to avoid slack stitches. As each loop becomes a stitch, you may have to pull on the thread a bit from underneath to get a smooth stitch. However, be sure to maintain an easy tension throughout your work; tight stitches will pucker the base fabric.

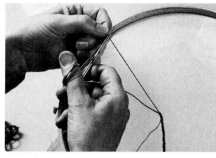

To end the chain stitch
Draw the last loop all the way through the previous one to lock it; then cut the yarn on the top side of the work (above.)

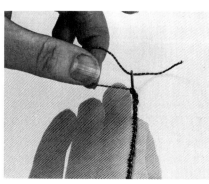

Using a tapestry needle, take the yarn to the back of the fabric just beyond the last chain stitch (above).

Using the tapestry needle, weave the end of the thread back through several stitches on the wrong side of the fabric (above).

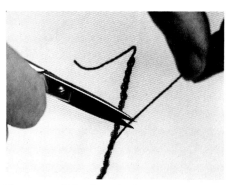

Then trim off the thread (above).

Working a design
To tambour a shape, outline the area with a single row of chain stitches; then fill in the shape by going round and round or back and forth within the outline. End the outline before you begin filling it in.

To do this, thread the yarn in a tapestry needle and pass it under the first stitch (above).

Insert the needle through the center of the last stitch, taking it to the back of the fabric (above). End the thread by weaving it back through several stitches, as before.

THE TAMBOUR STITCH

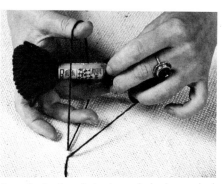

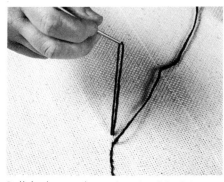

This gives a finished outline that forms a continuous chain (above).

If you are outlining several shapes and the distance between them is not great, you can move from one to the other without cutting the thread. To do this, insert the hook from back to front, and catch the last chain loop made (above).

Pull the loop to the underside of the fabric, making it large enough for the ball or skein of yarn to pass through (above).

Pass the ball or skein through the loop to lock the chain (above), and pull on the yarn to close it.

Working again on the top of the fabric, pull up a new loop to begin the new shape (above).

After all the elements of the design are completed, fill in the background.

Blocking your tambour work

If the tension of the stitches has puckered the base fabric or warped it, you will need to block it. Roll the work in a damp bath towel, then place it in a plastic bag until the entire piece is moist. Secure a bath towel to a board which is a few inches larger than your work. Place the embroidery face down on the towel. Stretch and smooth the handwork to shape it. As you do this, tack the fabric to the board around its edges. Tacks should be no more than one inch apart, and must be rustproof. If the completed embroidery is only rumpled, try steaming it. Fasten a thick bath towel to your ironing board (I do this with small safety pins and narrow elastic). Place the work face down on the towel. Cover it with a dampened towel; then steam with a warm iron. Never allow the weight of the iron to rest on the embroidery; hold it just close enough to produce a hissing sound.

Transferring your design

The tambour designs in the projects described here should be transferred directly onto the background fabric. To do this, make a tracing-paper pattern; then transfer it to the fabric in one of several ways. Which is best depends on the fabric and whether or not the pattern will be repeated many times.

A hot-iron transfer pencil, usually available at needlecraft supply shops, can be used on smooth fabrics. To transfer the design, go over the lines with the transfer pencil, working on the wrong side of the tracing-paper pattern. Pin or tape the pattern on the fabric, transfer-pencil-side down; then iron the design onto the fabric.

Direct tracing can be used if the design is small and the fabric is sheer and a light color. Make a tracing-paper pattern; then darken the lines. Tape the pattern on a well-lighted window pane, and tape the fabric on top of the pattern. Trace the design onto the fabric, using a soft lead pencil or waterproof marking pen.

Dressmaker's carbon, usually used to transfer clothing construction details, can be used to transfer simple designs to smooth fabrics. Tack or tape the fabric, right side up, on a flat surface. Pin the pattern to the fabric on three sides and slip the carbon between them, face down. Using a hard lead pencil or pattern tracing wheel, trace the design onto the fabric. Lift up the open side occasionally to make sure the carbon is transferring well. Disadvantages of dressmaker's carbon are that it tends to fade as the work is handled, and it smudges the fabric.

Basting stitches should be used on heavy or textured fabrics. First, pin or baste the paper pattern in position on the right side of the fabric. Then carefully sew over the design lines, using thread of contrasting color. (Silk works well.) Tear the pattern from the fabric before you begin tambouring, and remove the basting stitches when you have finished.

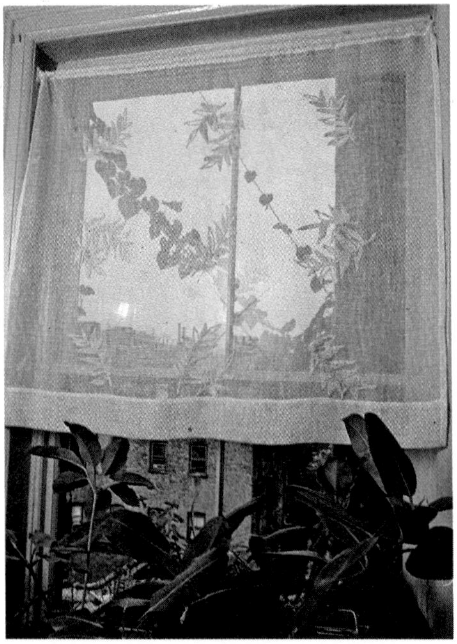

This gauze curtain, tamboured in the white-on-white tradition, illustrates how delicate tambour work can be. (The green leaves visible belong to an outdoor vine; they are not part of the curtain.)

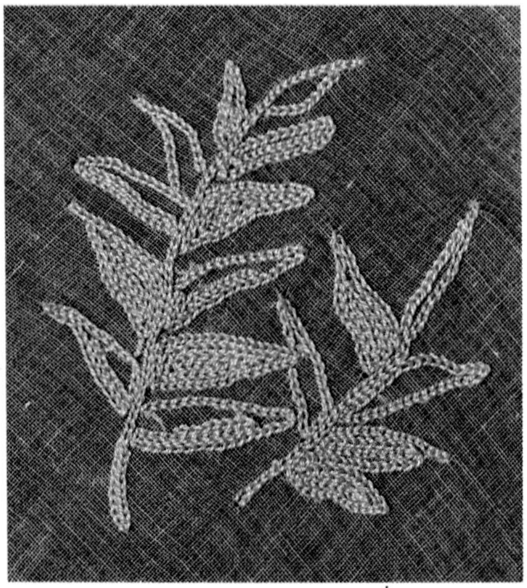

A close look at the white-on-white curtain reveals that some fronds are completely tamboured, but others are simply outlined, adding to the delicate, airy quality of the design.

Needlecrafts

White-on-white curtain

$ ● 🚶 ✂

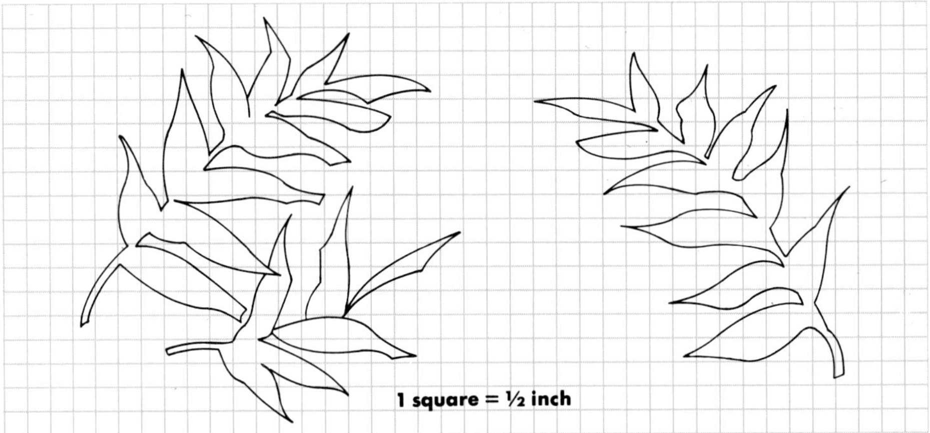

B

Figure B: To make patterns for the leaf designs used on the white-on-white curtain (left), enlarge these leaves by copying them, square by square, onto paper that you have ruled in ½-inch squares.

In the Victorian era, handworked linens and curtains gave homes a genteel touch of opulence. Through all the years since, hand-decorated curtains have retained their aura of luxury. One of the fastest and easiest ways to capture this touch is with tambour (top left).

The leaf patterns used to decorate this curtain are detailed in Figure B. You can use them as pictured, or adapt them to create a design of your own.

The materials you will need to make a curtain like this include nine skeins of No. 3 pearl cotton in off-white, and gauzy white curtain material, the amount depending on the size of your window. If you prefer, start with a ready-made curtain that has an open weave. You will also need a No. 4 or 5 crochet hook and an embroidery hoop large enough to accommodate one entire motif.

Enlarge the leaf designs (Figure B). Divide your curtain into nine equal sections, and transfer the design to the center of each section, using the direct tracing method (Craftnotes, page 2411). Alternate single and double leaves.

Stretch your fabric on a hoop, so that one complete motif shows within the hoop circle (Craftnotes, page 2409). When you work with a delicate fabric on a hoop, you can avoid distorting it by placing a strip of tissue paper over the bottom ring and taping it in place (photograph 3). Position the fabric over the hoop, and cover the edge with more tissue paper before you put on the top ring (photograph 4).

To tambour the leaves, refer to the Craftnotes, page 2410. As you finish each motif, center the next one in the hoop. When you have finished the tambour work, remove the curtain and steam it (Craftnotes, page 2411). By hand or machine, sew ¾-inch hems on the sides of the curtains and a 3-inch hem on the bottom. Then sew a casing on the top edges to fit your curtain rod.

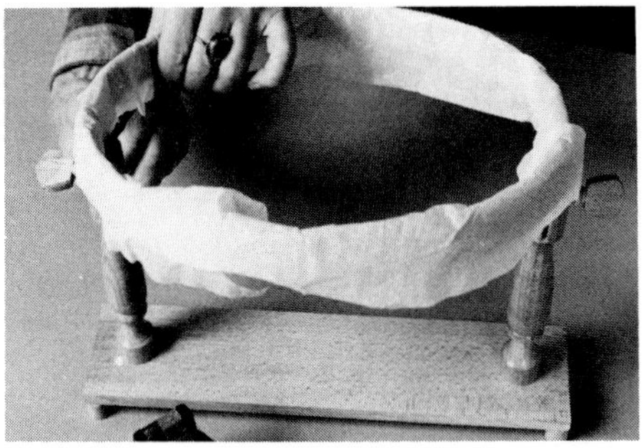

3: To keep a hoop from marking a delicate fabric, cushion the fabric by taping a strip of tissue paper onto the bottom ring.

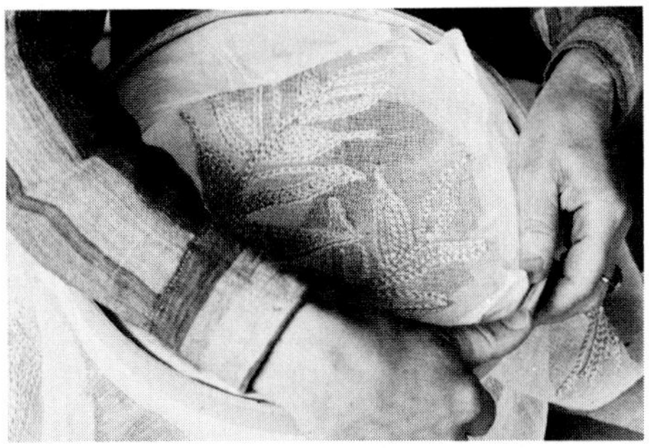

4: After you have placed the fabric over the bottom hoop, lay another strip of tissue paper around the edge before setting the top ring in place.

Needlecrafts
Banded wool rug

A banded wool rug with a wave design is not difficult to make. After you work the first row of tambour stitches in the middle of each band, repeat the same wavy line to fill in the area.

A handmade rug is a luxury indeed. The one shown above, perfect for keeping feet warm on a winter's night, is worked completely in tambour. Worked on firm monk's cloth, or burlap with strong rug yarn, it would withstand years of wear. But if you can't bear the thought of walking on such a rug, it can be used as a wall hanging.

The rug design consists of three bands, all based on the same curved line. To make it, you will need approximately 20 ounces of rya rug wool in all (I used leftover yarns in light blue, dark blue, olive green, and lavender for the top and bottom bands; off-white, gold, and gray for the middle band). In addition, you will need: a 40-inch square of a heavy open-weave fabric backing, such as monk's cloth; a 16-by-36-inch frame for stretching the fabric; a crochet or rug hook in an approximate size (I used a No. 0 hook); ball-point pens in two colors; ruler; and scissors. To finish the edges of the rug, you will need 4 yards of 1½-inch-wide twill tape rug binding, needle, and thread.

To begin, mark a 30-inch square in the center of the backing fabric with a ball-point pen. Divide and mark the 30-inch square into 3-inch squares. Then, using another color of ink, divide the 3-inch squares into 1-inch squares, forming a grid. Center the background fabric on the frame, and stretch it as described in the Craftnotes, page 2409.

The rug is worked freehand; there are no pattern lines to follow (the grid is used as a guide). The design consists of three 9-inch bands; in each band there is a series of

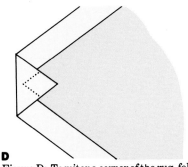

D

Figure D: To miter a corner of the rug, fold the point to the back, and clip corners as shown. The fold line should touch the corner of the tamboured design.

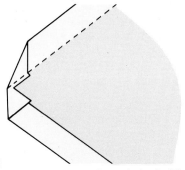

E

Figure E: Bring one edge to the back of the rug, folding it along the outer row of the tambour work.

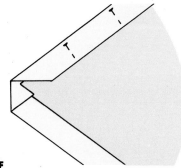

F

Figure F: Pin the folded edge in place.

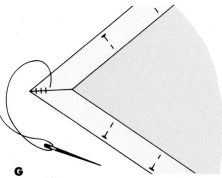

G

Figure G: Fold the other edge of the rug and pin it in place. Then, using needle and carpet sewing thread, stitch the diagonal at the corner.

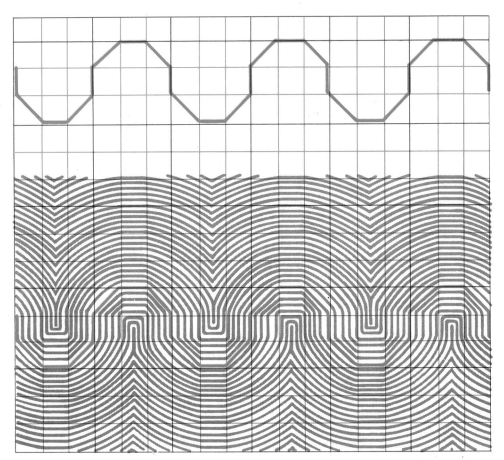

Figure C: To make the tamboured rug, mark a 30-inch square area at the center of the backing fabric and divide it into 3-inch squares with a ball-point pen (red lines). Then subdivide it into 1-inch squares (blue lines). Use these grid lines as your guide in placing the first row of each of the three 9-inch-wide bands of the design. Two colors are needed because the curve changes direction every 3 inches. Work the center row all the way across one band (top). Then fill in the rest of the band with rows of tambour, following the contours of that center row.

wavy stripes. Work one 9-inch band at a time, following the directions in the Craftnotes on page 2410. Work the center chain of the middle band first, starting on the left-hand side of the 30-inch square. Change the direction of the row as you reach each grid intersection, as indicated in Figure C, and continue tambouring until you reach the right-hand side of the marked square. Work the remaining rows of the band both above and below the first row, following its contours as closely as possible. To achieve the shaded effect shown in the middle band, arrange the colors so they graduate from light to dark. Work the top and bottom bands in the same way, establishing the center row first. Use this as a guide for filling in the rest. Move the fabric on the frame so that one whole band can be worked at a time.

When the entire 30-inch square has been tamboured, work the border. Make

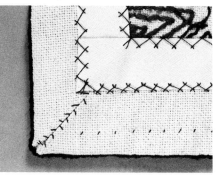

H

Figure H: Tack down the raw edge of the rug backing with catch stitches.

5: To finish the edges of the rug, place twill tape over them, and catch stitch the tape in place.

stripes of different colors, as I did, or use a solid color. Begin each row of the border in one corner and work around the perimeter of the square until you reach the starting corner. Then join the last chain stitch to the first chain stitch, forming an unending chain (Craftnotes, page 2410). Make the first border row next to the design area, then continue working rows of chain stitch until the border is 1½ inches wide.

Remove the finished rug from the frame and block or steam it into shape (Craftnotes, page 2411). To finish the edges, miter the corners, folding back the excess fabric in the process (Figures D, E, F, and G). Sew the hem flat with a catch stitch (Figure H). In order to keep the edges of the hem from fraying, sew the twill tape over them, again using a catch stitch (photograph 5).

Needlecrafts
Wall hanging

$ ● ♀ ☕

For those who like animals and have a penchant for needlework, the blue-cat wall hanging at right, adapted from the Caswell carpet, may be just the thing to liven up a wall. The cat takes a good amount of time to make, even if you are quite adept at tambouring, but it is fairly easy to do well. For it, you will need wool tapestry yarn, either in the colors shown (off-white, light blue, medium blue, and navy blue) or those of your choice. (This is a good place to use leftover yarn.) Other materials you need are: approximately ¾ yard of medium-weight striped fabric; an embroidery hoop or canvas-stretcher frame; four 17-inch canvas-stretcher strips assembled into a mounting frame; a staple gun and staples, or a hammer and tacks.

Enlarge the design for the cat (Figure I). Refer to the Craftnotes (pages 2410 and 2411) for instructions on transferring the design, tambouring, and blocking the finished piece. Make sure the design is centered on the fabric; then transfer the pattern lines to the fabric using basting stitches or transfer pencils. Stretch the

This wall hanging was adapted from one of the many motifs in the Caswell carpet, an early American folk embroidery that is on display at the Metropolitan Museum of Art in New York. This motif has inspired at least one story for children, *The Blue Cat*.

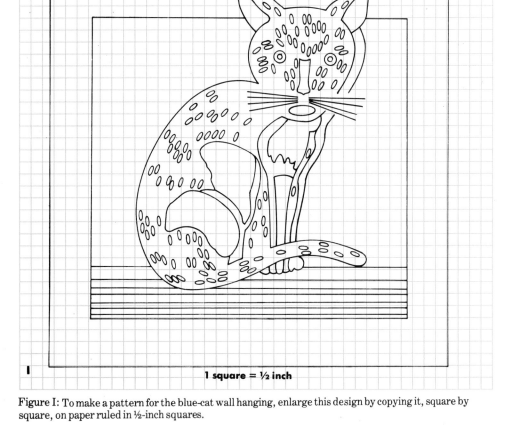

1 square = ½ inch

Figure I: To make a pattern for the blue-cat wall hanging, enlarge this design by copying it, square by square, on paper ruled in ½-inch squares.

fabric on the frame or in the hoop. To tambour the design, work the outline of the cat first; then fill in the details. Finally, work the borders. Remove the completed piece from the frame or hoop and block if necessary.

To mount the finished work, place it face down on a flat surface. Cover it with cardboard, and center the 17-inch-square frame on top. Temporarily tack or staple the fabric to the edges of the frame, working from the center of each side out to the corners. Trim the fabric diagonally at the corners if it is too bulky to make a neat fold. Staple or tack the edges to the back of the frame; then remove the temporary staples or tacks around the edges.

Needlecrafts
A leafy pillow

The lush, leafy design of the 15-by-18-inch pillow pictured below, like the blue cat on page 2415, was inspired by a motif in the Caswell carpet. Beautifully balanced in color and form, such a pillow could become an heirloom. You will need: wool tapestry yarn in off-white, peach, yellow, bronze, and bright blue; a piece of open-weave fabric, one 19-by-26-inch piece for the pillow front and a 16-by-19-inch piece for the back; polyester stuffing; a sewing needle and sewing thread to match the fabric; a crochet hook of an appropriate size (Craftnotes, page 2409); and an embroidery hoop or frame.

Enlarge the design for the pillow front (Figure J). Directions for transferring the design to fabric are given on page 2411. Using whichever method is best suited to your fabric, center the design on the larger piece and transfer the pattern lines. Stretch the fabric on a frame or hoop. Following the instructions on page 2410, tambour the design, first outlining, then filling in one area at a time.

When you have finished the tambour work, remove the fabric from the frame or hoop and block if necessary (Craftnotes, page 2411). To make the pillow, trim the

The rich texture and colors of Indian crewelwork, as pictured on page 2407, are reflected in this modern leafy pillow tamboured with wool tapestry yarn.

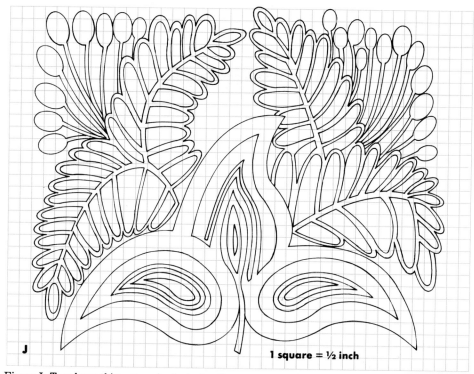

Figure J: To enlarge this pattern for the leafy pillow cover, copy the design, square by square, on paper that you have ruled in ½-inch squares.

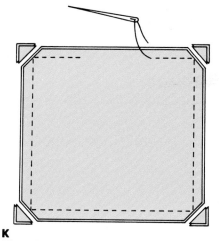

Figure K: After you have stitched the back and front of the pillow together, trim the corners on the diagonal, as shown. Turn the pillow right side out, stuff it, then hand stitch the opening closed.

pillow front to measure 16 by 19 inches. Place the front and back pieces of fabric together, right sides facing. Stitch together all around, making a ½-inch seam, but leave a 6-inch opening on one side for turning the pillow right side out (Figure K). Turn the pillow and fill it with polyester stuffing, being careful to pack the corners firmly. Fold the edges of the opening ½ inch to the inside, and sew it closed by hand with tiny stitches.

Needlecrafts
Dragonfly symbol

$ ● 🚶 🎇

The design shown at right was inspired by oriental lore, in which the dragonfly is a symbol of summer and a beneficent creature.

Delicate but vibrant with strong colors, this medallion can be used to decorate a vest (as pictured), a jacket, a kimono, or almost any other garment.

The materials you will need are: a 14¼-inch square of leaf-green cotton fabric; ½ yard of 36-inch-wide orange sailcloth or similar fabric; fusible web (available at sewing centers) that you can use to join the fabrics with an iron; scraps of white cotton net for the wings; 1-inch-wide bias tape in orange; polyester batting; interfacing; ruler; compass; scissors; iron; needle; straight-stitch or zigzag sewing machine; transfer pencil; straight pins; a crochet hook; and an embroidery hoop or frame. For tambouring, you will need an assortment of threads and yarns. For the dragonfly design pictured, the following threads and colors were used: No. 5 pearl cotton in light, medium, and dark turquoise (for the body), light and dark gray (for the shadows and wing outlines), orange (for the border), and green (for the leaves); No. 3 pearl cotton in yellow and pink (for the border); thin black wool (for the legs); black silk machine thread (for outlining the head); white and gray buttonhole twist (for the wings); and white linen machine thread (for highlights).

To prepare the background fabric, enlarge the design given in Figure L, including the cross at the center which indicates the positioning of the dragonfly. Transfer this onto the green background fabric, following the instructions in the Craft-

Judy sewed the tamboured dragonfly motif on the back of her quilted vest. Yours could be stitched to a jacket, a dress, or a pillow.

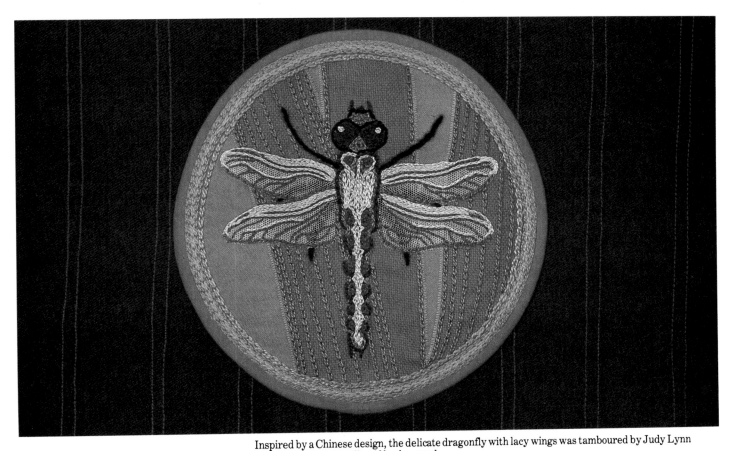

Inspired by a Chinese design, the delicate dragonfly with lacy wings was tamboured by Judy Lynn Pickett on a round appliquéd background.

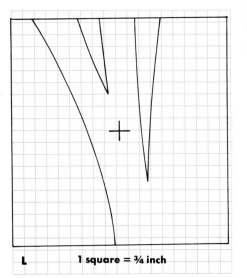

L   1 square = ¾ inch

Figure L: To make patterns for the rays of sunlight behind the dragonfly, enlarge this design on a 14¼-inch square of paper that you have ruled in ¾-inch squares. Copy the shapes, square by square, onto the larger grid; then mark the center of the paper pattern with a cross as indicated. These rays will be appliquéd to the background fabric.

notes, page 2411. Cut out the orange areas of the pattern. Pin them to the orange sailcloth on the bias; then cut them out. Cut pieces of the fusible web, using the same patterns. Position the sailcloth sunlight pieces on the green background fabric with fusible web between the two. Then iron the fabrics together following the directions on the web package. Outline the edges of the orange pieces with yellow thread, using a straight or zigzag stitch.

Trace the patterns for the dragonfly body and wings (Figure M). Using the transfer pencil method, iron the dragonfly pattern lines on the background fabric (Craftnotes, page 2411). Make sure your tracing is positioned so the crosses on both pieces are aligned. With a compass, mark two concentric circles around the dragonfly, one 7¼ inches in diameter, the other 8½ inches in diameter. These will form the border.

Stretch the fabric on the frame or in the hoop. Following the directions in the Craftnotes on page 2410, work each element of the design in the following sequence: Tambour the black legs first. Then cut out, pin, and baste the net wings in place (they will overlap the legs). Next, tambour the body and head, the wings, the border, and finally, the leaf veins. Refer to the pattern and the color photograph.

When all the tambouring is done, remove the work from the hoop or frame, and block or steam it back into shape (Craftnotes, page 2411).

To finish the appliqué, use a compass to make a 10-inch paper circle. Center it over the symbol, and cut the circle from the square background. Use the same patterns to cut a circle from orange sailcloth for the backing. Make an 8-inch-diameter circular pattern, and use it to cut the batting and interfacing. Using catch stitches (Figure H, page 2414), temporarily sew first the interfacing and then the batting to the back of the design. With a soft pencil, center and draw a circular seam line 8½ inches in diameter on the back of the medallion. With right sides facing, pin the sailcloth backing to the symbol, and machine stitch them together on the seam line. Make sure you avoid catching any of the tamboured border in the seam. Trim the seam to ¼ inch. Make a slit about 3 inches long in the backing, and turn the symbol

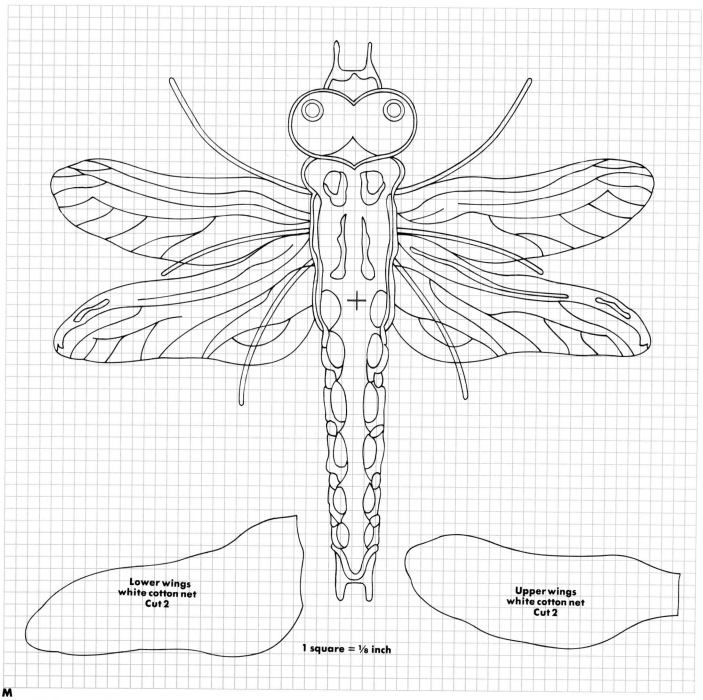

Lower wings
white cotton net
Cut 2

Upper wings
white cotton net
Cut 2

1 square = ⅛ inch

M

Figure M: To make patterns for the dragonfly body, which will be worked in tambour, and the upper and lower wings, which are cut from cotton net, enlarge both elements on paper that you have ruled in ⅛-inch squares. Copy the designs, square by square; then mark the center of the dragonfly with a cross so you can transfer the pattern to the background fabric in the correct position.

right side out through the slit. Press it according to the directions in the Craftnotes, page 2411. Sew the slit closed by hand and remove the catch stitches.

To make the orange border, open out one folded edge of the bias tape. With the raw edge on the perimeter of the circle, pin the tape to the edge of the medallion, right sides facing. Machine stitch the tape to the medallion along the crease; then turn the bias tape to the back of the medallion, and sew the edge in place by hand. With matching thread, hand stitch the medallion to the garment of your choice.

For related crafts and entries, see "Appliqué," "Crewelwork Sampler," "Crochet," "Embroidery," and "Hooked Rugs."

TATTING

A Different Kind of Lace

Josephine Mayer of New York learned needlecrafts from her grandmother in Prague, Czechoslovakia, and she could crochet before she could write. She received her Ph.D. degree in mathematics in Prague and served as a biophysicist at Mount Sinai Hospital in New York after her arrival in the United States in 1942. She combines both interests by teaching mathematics and needlecrafts to children who have learning difficulties. She often prepares knitting and crochet designs for magazines. Josie has a daughter and two grandchildren; her granddaughter models a vest on page 2426.

The French call it *frivolité,* while English-speaking countries, perhaps being less frivolous, call it tatting. The term describes a type of lace made almost entirely of knots, worked with a shuttle as a tool. (Other familiar types of lace include bobbin lace, made by crossing and twisting—but not knotting—threads wound on bobbins, and needle lace, worked with a needle in embroiderylike stitches, one of which is knotting.)

The tatting shuttle (page 2424) is made of two outside pieces, each tapered at both ends, held together by a midsection—either an attached post or a removable bobbin—around which the tatting thread is wound. The tapered ends very nearly touch, in order that the thread will not unwind unintentionally. There may be a point or hook at one end, useful for picking out mistakes and joining pieces.

The shuttle, with thread wound in place, is passed over and under a ring of thread wrapped around one hand. These movements create a series of knots called stitches and loops called picots. These stitches and picots can be joined to form rings, semicircles, chains, and bars. A huge variety of designs, both flat and three-dimensional, is possible with different arrangements of these motifs.

Tatting originated in Europe as a technique of first knotting the threads, then couching these strings of knots onto fabric in an intricate design. During the Victorian era, tatting evolved into its present form and it became quite popular for use in handkerchief and pillowcase edgings, round doilies, and tablecloths. The thread used was almost always thin white or ecru cotton, so the tatting had a delicate, fragile look. Prominent women especially liked the beauty of tatting, and several paintings of the time show them tatting with gold or silver shuttles.

Tatting is becoming popular again, partly because of the current interest in things of the past, and partly because contemporary ideas are being expressed and modern materials are being tried. Tatting now includes, in addition to traditional choices, garments made of tatting and functional household items made with soft, thick yarns in a rainbow of colors. Projects that follow include a handkerchief edging, a collar, a vest, a place mat, a plant hanger, and a tablecloth.

Perhaps the most traditional use for tatting is in making a dainty white edging for a crisp white handkerchief. The edging on the wedding handkerchief, left, consists of a 5-inch band of very delicate rings, loosely joined together. The hemstitched handkerchief, center, has a similar edging, done with slightly thicker thread and larger rings. The more tailored handkerchief, right, has a narrower scalloped edging; yet the motifs again consist of rings and picots.

Opposite: This cloverleaf handkerchief edging is recommended for a novice tatter. The motifs are simply rings of double stitches and picots, the two basic stitches in tatting; yet the variegated thread gives the design an intricate look. Directions begin on page 2424.

Winding the shuttle

If your shuttle has a removable bobbin, wind the thread on it; then snap the bobbin into place. If the shuttle is all one piece, hold the end of the thread with your thumb against the edge of the shuttle and wind the thread around the post in the center. If there is a hole in the center of the post, ignore it. It is often suggested that you put the thread through the hole and knot it, but this is unnecessary and time-consuming, especially when you reach the end of the thread and must unknot it. Do not wind the thread beyond the edges of the shuttle; if you do, the thread is likely to become soiled and worn from repeated passage through your hands.

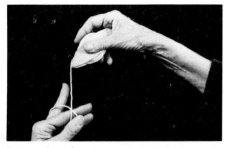

Preparing the ring and shuttle threads

With your right hand (if you are right-handed), hold the shuttle horizontally. (If you are left-handed, hold a mirror to the left of each photograph to see the correct working position.) If the shuttle has a point or hook, that end should face forward, out of your hand. Unwind about 15 inches of shuttle thread; it should be unwinding from the back of the shuttle that is nearer the palm of your right hand. Take the free end of the thread, holding it several inches from the end between the thumb and index finger of your left hand. Spread and bend the other fingers of that hand, as much as is comfortable, and make a circle of the thread over the back and under those fingers. Bring the thread back between your thumb and index finger and hold securely at the point where the thread crosses itself.

Hold the middle finger of your left hand high to keep the circle of the thread open. The shuttle will be passed between your middle and index fingers and your middle and ring fingers; the middle finger must be raised high enough for the shuttle to pass comfortably between those fingers. Stretch the shuttle thread out horizontally, keeping both hands at the same level.

The thread around your left hand is called the ring thread, but do not confuse it with the term **ring** which refers to a tatted ring of stitches. You will hold the ring thread closed, without letting go, until both parts of the first knot have been made. The thread coming from your right hand is called the shuttle thread.

The most important thing to remember about all tatting stitches is that the stitch always ends up with the ring thread knotted onto the shuttle thread. For the beginner, the temptation is to do the reverse, making the knots with the shuttle thread. In fact, as you start a stitch, you do make a knot with the shuttle thread. You must then snap the shuttle thread taut as you relax the ring thread in order to reverse the knotted and knot-bearing threads. You will know you have made the knot correctly if it slides easily along the shuttle thread. If you make a mistake, the knot will not move and you will need to unpick it with the point of the shuttle, a needle, or a fine crochet hook before you can continue.

The double stitch

This basic tatting knot is worked in two parts. There are several ways of making this knot, all resulting in the same stitch; I think this way is the simplest, though not the usual.

The first half

Loop the shuttle thread over the back of your left hand, from the thumb past the middle finger. Then pass the shuttle over the back of the ring thread, pointing it toward your left palm. Next, bring it under the front of the ring thread, between your middle and index fingers. Pass the shuttle between the ring thread and the beginning loop made around the back of the hand.

Take the shuttle thread back to the right, pulling it taut with a jerk, and at the same time, relax the middle finger of your left hand so that the first half of the knot switches from the shuttle thread onto the ring thread where it belongs. If you practice this with a heavy cord, as shown, you can see this happen. For practice, you can re-

peatedly transfer a loosely made knot back and forth between threads.

Now, raise your middle finger high to slide the loop into place between your thumb and index finger, and to open the ring thread circle in preparation for the second half of the double stitch. Take the shuttle back to its original position, in line with your left hand so the shuttle thread is horizontal.

The second half

Without wrapping the thread around either hand, take the shuttle directly toward the back of the left hand, and pass it under the back of the ring thread. Pass it from back to front through the center of the ring thread circle between your middle and ring fingers.

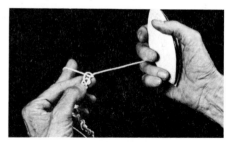

Again, relax the middle finger of the left hand and snap the shuttle thread taut so that it becomes the knot-bearer, with the ring thread forming the second half of the double knot. Raise your middle finger to slide the loop into place, between thumb and forefinger of the left hand, and return the shuttle to its original position.

Check to be sure that the knot slides easily back and forth over the shuttle thread, and that the size of the ring thread circle can be easily adjusted. It is a good idea to keep checking this as work proceeds.

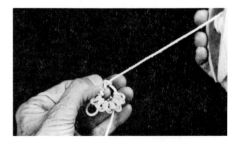

TATTING STITCHES

Making a ring of tatted stitches (photograph at bottom of opposite page)

Make the desired number of double stitches. Hold the last stitch firmly between the thumb and index finger of your left hand and draw up the shuttle thread with your right hand. Slide the stitches along the shuttle thread until the first and last stitches meet, closing the ring.

Making picots

The little loops called picots are used for decoration and for joining rings of stitches. Picots are made only between whole knots, not between the halves of the double stitch.

Leave a short length of thread between the two double stitches. The length will be determined by your design, the size of the thread, and whether it will be used for joining.

As the stitch following the picot is slid into place on the shuttle thread, the extra length of thread will create the loop. With practice, you will be able to make even picots.

Joinings

A ring (or chain) of tatted stitches can be joined to a preceding ring by means of a picot on the first ring.

Make the desired number of stitches in the second ring, up to the joining point.

Insert the point of the shuttle (or a crochet hook) through the indicated picot of the first ring and catch the ring thread that is on your left hand. Through the picot, draw a loop large enough for the shuttle to pass through.

Pass the shuttle through the loop and pull the shuttle thread taut.

At the same time, raise the middle finger of your left hand to draw up the ring thread, thus joining the two rings and making the first half of the next double stitch.

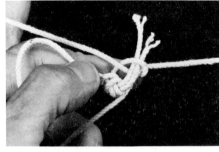

Attaching a new thread

When you have nearly reached the end of your shuttle thread, leave a tail of an inch or so and hold this end together with the beginning of the new shuttle thread. Work the first half of the double stitch over both ends. This may be a bit bulky with heavy yarns, but is barely noticeable with thinner threads.

Then work the second half of the double stitch over both ends. Try to start a new thread in an inconspicuous place and in a double stitch, not in a picot. Include the ends in as many stitches as necessary to secure them, or whipstitch the remaining ends to the tatted stitches with sewing thread of a matching color.

Using ball and shuttle threads

Tatting designs often contain chains, as well as rings and picots. Chains are made with the thread wound halfway around the left hand, instead of in a circle as for rings. When rings and chains appear in the same design, you will need two working threads, the shuttle thread previously described and a ball thread.

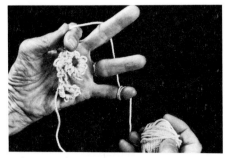

When a ring is completed and drawn up, and a chain is about to be made, turn the ring so that the base of it is at the top, and hold it between your left thumb and index finger. This is called **reverse work**.

Tie the end of the ball thread to the shuttle thread; then wrap the ball thread over the back of your fingers and wind it around your little finger to control the tension.

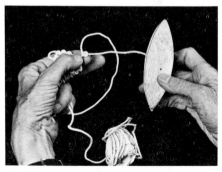

Work the chain of double knots over the ball thread with the shuttle thread, just as you did for making rings. When you have finished the chain, slide the stitches close together and put down the ball thread. Reverse the work (putting the base of the previous ring at the bottom again) and pick up the shuttle thread. Work the next ring with the shuttle thread.

Using two shuttles and a ball thread

When rings are worked in two colors and chains in a third, two shuttles and a ball thread are used. To alternate shuttle colors, put down the shuttle used to make the last ring and pick up the second shuttle, then work the next ring as usual. The chains are worked with the ball thread knotted onto the shuttle thread of the preceding ring.

Shuttles
Right: Over the centuries, the tatting shuttle has changed very little. In the center is a long netting shuttle that can be used for yarn. Reading clockwise from its point, the tatting shuttles are: an antique engraved-silver shuttle; a modern plastic one-piece shuttle, sold in variety stores and needlecraft shops; a handmade balsawood shuttle for thick yarn (see Craftnotes, page 2430, for directions); an antique tortoise-shell shuttle; a shuttle dating from the 1920s; a well-used silver shuttle; a tiny ivory shuttle; and a steel shuttle with a removable bobbin that can be wound separately, then snapped into place.

Abbreviations used
ds	Double stitch
P	Picot
()	Do what is indicated between parentheses the number of times specified.

This detail photograph shows one cloverleaf of the handkerchief edging pictured on page 2421.

Weaving, Braiding, and Knotting
Handkerchief edging

The handkerchief edging pictured at left and on page 2421, could also be used to trim lingerie, a pocket or sleeve, or even doll clothes. It is ½ inch deep.
Materials: One ball of variegated crochet cotton, size 10, and a tatting shuttle.

Directions
First cloverleaf
Ring 1 (small): 12 ds, P, 6 ds, P, 6 ds; close.
Ring 2 (large): 6 ds, join to last P of previous ring, (6 ds, P) 4 times, 6 ds; close.
Ring 3 (small): 6 ds, join to last P of previous ring, 6 ds, P, 12 ds; close.

Leave about 1 inch of thread connecting the first and second cloverleaves.

Second cloverleaf
Ring 1 (small): 12 ds, join to last P of third ring of previous cloverleaf, 6 ds, P, 6 ds; close.
Rings 2 and 3: Work as in first cloverleaf. Repeat second cloverleaf to within 1½ inches of required length, leaving a 1-inch connecting thread between cloverleaves.

Final cloverleaf
Rings 1 and 2: Work as in second cloverleaf.
Ring 3 (small): 6 ds, join to last P of previous ring, 6 ds, join to first P of first cloverleaf. Break off.
Finishing: Sew the edging onto the handkerchief by hand or machine. Starch lightly, and press carefully.

Weaving, Braiding, and Knotting
Shell-cluster collar

The collar on the opposite page can be worn with the pointed ends toward the front, with the inner edge outlining a V-shaped neckline. Or it can be worn with the rounded back turned forward, following the curve of a shallow scoop neckline. The collar is 3½ inches wide.
Materials: One large ball of ecru mercerized crochet cotton, size 20, and a tatting shuttle.
Directions
Tie the ends of the ball and shuttle threads together (Craftnotes, page 2423).

Round 1 (inner edge)
Cluster motif 1
Ring 1 (with shuttle thread only): 5 ds, (P, ds) 5 times, P, 5 ds; close.

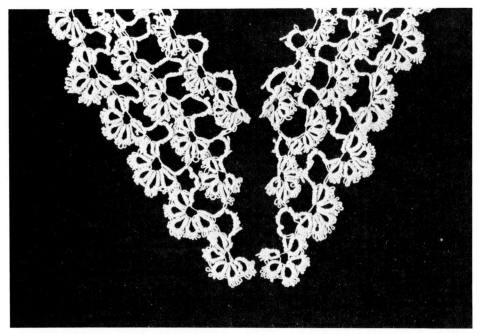

The collar, shown being worn backward in the photograph at the right, appears as shown above when it is worn with the pointed ends to the front; the inner edge can be sewn to a V-shaped neckline. The collar is made of three rows of clusters of rings, joined by undulating chains of double stitches and picots.

The shell-motif collar made of ecru crochet cotton can be worn backward to follow the curve of a shallow scoop neckline.

Rings 2 through 5: 5 ds, join to last P of previous ring, ds, (P, ds) 4 times, P, 5 ds; close.

Join last ring to base of first ring. Reverse work (Craftnotes, page 2423). *Chain 1* (with ball and shuttle threads): 4 ds, join to last P of last ring, (4 ds, P) 3 times, 4 ds.

Cluster motif 2
Ring 1: 5 ds, join to last P of previous chain, ds, join to last P of last ring of previous motif, ds, (P, ds) 3 times, P, 5 ds; close.
Rings 2 through 5: Work them as in cluster motif 1.
Chain 2: Work as in chain 1.

Cluster motifs 3 through 14
Work as in cluster motif 2.

Cluster motif 15
Work as in cluster motif 2, ending with ring 5—do not work chain.
Cut ends and fasten off.

Round 2
Cluster motif 1
Ring 1: 7 ds, (P, ds) 7 times, P, 7 ds; close.
Rings 2 through 5: 7 ds, join to last P of previous ring, ds, (P, ds) 6 times, P, 7 ds; close. Join last ring to base of first ring. Reverse work.
Chain 1: 6 ds, join to last P of previous ring, (6 ds, P) 4 times, 6 ds.

Cluster motif 2
Ring 1: 7 ds, join to last P of previous chain, ds, join to last P of last ring of previous motif, ds, (P, ds) 5 times, P, 7 ds; close.
Rings 2 through 5: Work as in cluster motif 1.
Chain 2: 6 ds, join to last P of previous ring, 6 ds, join to middle P of fourth ring of first cluster motif of previous round, 6 ds, P, 6 ds, join to middle P of second ring of second cluster motif of previous round, 6 ds, P, 6 ds.

Cluster motifs 3 through 15
Work as in cluster motif 2, joining each motif to the next motif of the previous round. End with ring 5 of motif 15—do not work chain. Cut ends.

Round 3
Cluster motif 1
Ring 1: 9 ds, (P, ds) 9 times, P, 9 ds; close.
Rings 2 through 5: 9 ds, join to last P of previous ring, ds, (P, ds) 8 times, P, 9 ds; close. Join last ring to base of first ring. Reverse work.
Chain 1: 8 ds, join to last P of previous ring, (8 ds, P) 5 times, 8 ds.

Cluster motif 2
Ring 1: 9 ds, join to last P of previous chain, ds, join to last P of last ring of previous motif, ds, (P, ds) 7 times, P, 9 ds; close.

Rings 2 through 5: Work them as in cluster motif 1.
Chain 2: 8 ds, join to last P of previous ring, 8 ds, join to middle P of fourth ring of first cluster motif of previous round, 8 ds, P, 8 ds, join to middle P of second ring of second cluster motif of previous round, 8 ds, P, 8 ds.

Cluster motifs 3 through 16
Work same as cluster motif 2, joining each motif to the next motif of the previous round. End with ring 5 of motif 16—do not work chain.
Finishing: Cut and tie ends; whipstitch. Starch lightly, if desired, and press on a padded surface. For the best results, insert nonrusting straight pins through the outer picots while pressing.

This close-up shows one shell-cluster motif of the lacy tatted collar.

Weaving, Braiding, and Knotting
Child's vest

¢ ⏱ 🚶 🧵

This is one square of the vest made of sock-and-sweater yarn, shown at the right.

Cynthia Palmer proudly models the tatted vest her grandmother made. Three crocheted buttons keep the vest closed.

The vest has a flare to it due to a decrease of two squares in the underarm row. The squares are similar to crocheted granny squares.

Soft, brightly colored yarn, an untraditional choice for tatting, can be used quite successfully for making a young girl's vest. These tricolored squares of tatting resemble crocheted granny squares, but they have a more delicate and feminine look.

Size: The child's size-10 vest is made of 35 squares. The size can be adjusted by adding or subtracting squares.

Materials: Sock and sweater yarn (2 ounce skeins)—1 dark turquoise, 1 orange, and 2 ivory; plus two tatting shuttles.

Directions
Wind one shuttle with turquoise yarn and one with orange. Wind the ivory into a ball—this will be used to make all of the chains.

One square
Round 1 (orange shuttle)
Starting in the center of the square, make a ring of (P, 3 ds) 8 times; close. Tie ends, cut, and whipstitch.

Round 2 (turquoise shuttle and ivory ball)
Ring 1 (inner): 4 ds, join to any P of center ring, 4 ds; close.
Chain 1: 2 ds, P, 2 ds.
Ring 2 (small outer): 4 ds, P, 4 ds; close.
Chain 2: Repeat chain 1.
Ring 3 (inner): 4 ds, join to next P of center ring, 4 ds; close.
Chain 3: Repeat chain 1.
Ring 4 (large outer): 4 ds, (P, ds) 5 times, 3 ds; close.
Chain 4: Repeat chain 1.
These four rings and four chains complete one-quarter of round 2 of the square. Repeat in the same order three more times. Tie the ends to the beginning of this round.
Round 3 (orange shuttle and ivory ball).
Ring 1: 3 ds, join to first P of any large outer ring, 3 ds; close.
Chain 1: 2 ds, P, 2 ds.
Ring 2: 5 ds, join to second P of same large outer ring, 5 ds; close.
Chain 2: Repeat chain 1.
Ring 3: 7 ds, join to third P of same large outer ring, 7 ds; close.
Chain 3: Repeat chain 1.
Ring 4: 5 ds, join to fourth P of same large outer ring, 5 ds; close.

Chain 4: Repeat chain 1.
Ring 5: 3 ds, join to fifth P of same large outer ring, 3 ds; close.
Chain 5: Repeat chain 1.
Ring 6: 4 ds, join to P of next small outer ring, 4 ds; close.
Chain 6: Repeat chain 1.
Ring 7: 4 ds, join to same P as ring 6, 4 ds; close.
Chain 7: Repeat chain 1.
These seven rings and seven chains complete one-quarter of round 3 of the square. Repeat in order three more times. Tie ends to the beginning of this round. This completes one square.

Remainder of the squares
Work as the first square, except instead of making picots in the chains of round 3, join to the picots on the sides of other squares.

Join the squares as they are completed in the order shown in Figure A.

Finishing: Sew three crocheted or purchased buttons evenly spaced along the edge of the top square on the left side. To close, push the buttons through openings in the corresponding square on the right side as pictured.

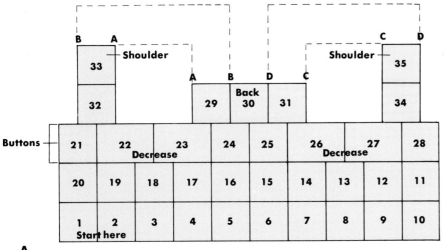

A

Figure A: On the last round of each square, join it to the neighboring square or squares, as shown. Join ten squares for each of the first two rows, starting at the bottom of the vest and following the numerical sequence given. Decrease the number of squares in the third row to eight by easing two squares to fit three squares in the previous row as indicated. In the fourth row, start the end squares at the midpoints of the end squares in the previous row. In the same row, skip the width of one square for each armhole, and stagger the three back squares over the four center back squares of the previous row. Join the shoulder squares to the two end squares of the center back as shown.

Weaving, Braiding, and Knotting
Sunflower place mat

¢ ● 🧍 🧶

You are sure to set a sunny table with a set of sunflower place mats in vibrant colors. This one was tatted with a medium-weight crochet cotton. Each sunflower is edged with green to form a square; these squares are joined and edged with a ruffle of tatted rings.

The circle-in-a-square design of this ruffled table mat is quite contemporary; yet it would harmonize with all but a formal style of decorating.
Size: 15 inches wide by 22 inches long overall; each sunflower section is 7 inches square.

Materials: Medium-weight 3-ply mercerized crochet cotton thread (2 balls of avocado, 1 ball of tango orange, and 1 ball of dark yellow), and a tatting shuttle.

Directions for one square

First, using tango orange

Round 1
Starting in the center of the flower, with the shuttle thread only, make a ring of (2 ds, P) 8 times; close. Tie ends, cut, and whipstitch.

Round 2
(Motifs radiating from the center ring)
Motif 1
Chain 1: 2 ds, join to any P of center ring, 2 ds. Reverse work.
Ring 1: 2 ds, P, (ds, P) 3 times, 2 ds; close.

Motifs 2 through 7
Work as in motif 1, except join each ring to P of previous ring, instead of making first P.

Motif 8
Work as in motifs 2 through 7, except join to first P of first ring, instead of making final P. Tie ends to the beginning of the round; cut off ends.

Next, using dark yellow
(Tie shuttle and ball threads together.)

Round 3 (Yellow petals)
Motif 1
Ring 1: 2 ds, join to any available P in previous round, 2 ds; close.
Chain 1: 4 ds.
Ring 2: 2 ds, P, 2 ds; close.
Chain 2: 4 ds.

Motifs 2 through 32
Work as in motif 1, joining the first ring of each motif to a successive P of the previous round. Tie ends to the beginning of the round; cut off ends.

Finally, using avocado green
(Tie shuttle and ball threads together.)

Round 4 (one side of square)
Ring 1: 8 ds, join to a corner P of previous round, 8 ds; close.
Chain 1: 3 ds, P, 3 ds.
Ring 2: Work as in ring 1, joining to the same P of the previous round to make a corner of the square.
Chain 2: 2 ds, P, 2 ds.
Ring 3: 6 ds, join to next P of previous round, 6 ds; close.
Chain 3: 2 ds, P, 2 ds.
Ring 4: 4 ds, join to next P of previous round, 4 ds; close.
Chain 4: 2 ds, P, 2 ds.
Ring 5: 2 ds, join to next P of previous round, 2 ds; close.
Chain 5: 2 ds, P, 2 ds.
Ring 6: 1 ds, join to next P of previous round, ds; close.
Chain 6: 2 ds, P, 2 ds.
Ring 7: 2 ds, join to next P of previous round, 2 ds; close.
Chain 7: 2 ds, P, 2 ds.
Ring 8: 4 ds, join to next P of previous round, 4 ds; close.
Chain 8: 2 ds, P, 2 ds.
Ring 9: 6 ds, join to next P of previous round, 6 ds; close.
Chain 9: 2 ds, P, 2 ds.

This is a detail of one sunflower square and the ruffled edging of the place mat shown on page 2427.

These nine rings and nine chains make up the first row of one side of the square surrounding the sunflower. Repeat them for the other three sides, with rings 1 and 2 worked in the same picot of the previous round to form the corners. Tie ends to the beginning of the round; cut off ends and whipstitch.

Round 5 (one side of square)
Ring 1, starting at a corner: 4 ds, P, 4 ds, join to corresponding P of previous round, 4 ds, P, 4 ds; close.
Chain 1: 2 ds, P, 2 ds.
Ring 2: 4 ds, join to last P of previous ring, 4 ds, join to same P of previous round as ring 1, 4 ds, P, 4 ds; close.
Chain 2: 2 ds, P, 2 ds.
Ring 3: Work as in ring 2 (3 rings made in one P of previous round at the corner).
Chain 3: 2 ds, P, 2 ds.
Rings 4 through 11: Work as in ring 2, but join each ring to successive P of previous round.
Chains 4 through 11: 2 ds, P, 2 ds.
These 11 rings and 11 chains make up the second row of one side of the square. Repeat for the other three sides. At each corner there will be three rings joined to the same picot of a chain of the previous round. Tie ends to beginning of round; cut off ends, and whipstitch.

The remaining five squares
Work as in the first square, arranging the squares three across and two down. Join each square to the adjoining square by replacing the P in the outer chains with *the corresponding P of the last round of the previous square.*

The ruffled edging
Using avocado green, tie the shuttle and ball threads together. Start at one corner with *Motif 1:*
Ring 1: (P, ds) 8 times, 8 ds; close.
Ring 2: 8 ds, join to last P of previous ring, ds, (P, ds) 7 times; close.
Chain 1: 4 ds.

Motifs 2 through 32
Work as in motif 1, joining each motif to successive P of previous round. Tie ends to the beginning of the round; cut and whipstitch.
Finishing: Starch place mat lightly, if desired. Then press carefully on a padded surface, inserting nonrusting straight pins through the picots on the outer edge for the best results.

Weaving, Braiding and Knotting
Flowerpot holder

This is a detail of the flowerpot holder shown at the left.

You can hang a favorite trailing plant in this tatted cover made of rug yarn. Because the yarn is thick, you need to use a netting shuttle or a large handmade balsa-wood shuttle.

Two earthy colors of thick rug yarn alternate in horizontal bands in this hanging flowerpot cover. A copper color is used as the shuttle thread, making all of the rings, while a natural color is used for all but the first round of the diagonal bars of chain stitches that are worked over the shuttle thread (Craftnotes, page 2423). Due to the thickness of the yarn, you will need to use a netting shuttle or an extra-large balsa-wood shuttle (Craftnotes, page 2430).

Size: This holder fits a flowerpot approximately 7½ inches in diameter and 8 inches high. It can be adjusted to fit other sizes by changing the number of rounds or the number of rings and chains in each round.

Materials: Rug yarn (1 skein of copper, 2 skeins of natural), and one large netting or tatting shuttle. (Natural-color yarn can be wound into a small ball.)

Directions
(starting at the bottom of the cover)

Round 1 (copper rings and chains, on the bottom of the pot)
Ring 1: (6 ds, P) 3 times, 6 ds; close.
Chain 1: 6 ds, P, 6 ds.
Rings 2, 3, and 4: 6 ds, join to last P of previous ring, 6 ds, P, 6 ds, P, 6 ds; close.

Chains 2, 3 and 4: 6 ds, join to P of previous chain, 6 ds.
Ring 5: 6 ds, join to last P of previous ring, 6 ds, P, 6 ds, join to first P of first ring, 6 ds; close.
Chain 5: 6 ds, join to P of previous chain, 6 ds. Tie ends to the beginning of the round; cut off ends.
Round 2 (copper rings and natural chains).
This is an increase round. Join every three rings in this round to the three available picots of one ring in the previous round.

Ring 1: 6 ds, P, 6 ds, join to any available P of previous round, 6 ds, P, 6 ds; close.

2429

Chain 1: 6 ds, P, 6 ds.
Rings 2 through 14: 6 ds, join to last P of previous ring, 6 ds, join to next available P of previous round, 6 ds, P, 6 ds; close.
Chains 2 through 14: 6 ds, P, 6 ds.
Ring 15: 6 ds, join to last P of previous ring, 6 ds, join to next available P of previous round, 6 ds, join to first P of first ring, 6 ds; close.
Chain 15: 6 ds, P, 6 ds. Tie ends to the beginning of the round; cut off ends.

Rounds 3 and 4 (copper rings and natural chains)
Work as in round 2, except join each ring to a picot of a chain of the previous round instead of to a picot of a ring. No increases will be made.
Finishing: Make five hanging cords of the desired length by twisting together eight lengths of natural yarn for each cord. Knot the cords together at the top, or wrap and tie them with a separate piece of yarn. Weave the cords

through openings in the cover, spacing them evenly. Knot the cords together at the bottom of the cover, leaving several inches of the ends to make a tassel.

Thread a double thickness of natural-colored yarn through the chains of the last round, and gather the cover over the pot to fit snugly. Tie the yarn in a knot that can be loosened, if necessary, to remove the plant for periodic care.

The cover can be lightly starched and shaped over the pot, if desired.

CRAFTNOTES: MAKING A LARGE SHUTTLE

To do contemporary tatting with cords and yarns, you can use the kind of netting shuttle that you can buy (page 2424), or you can make a large tatting shuttle of lightweight balsa wood.

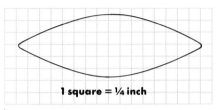

1 square = ¼ inch

To make the balsa-wood shuttle, enlarge the pattern above. Draw a grid of ¼-inch squares on paper and redraw the outline of the shuttle side, square by square. Trace this shape twice onto ⅜-inch-thick balsa wood and outline it with a felt-tipped waterproof marker. (You will need a piece of wood about 1 foot long and 2 or 3 inches wide.)

Using a single-edged razor blade carefully, whittle away the excess wood to get the curved shuttle shape. This wood is soft and easy to cut, but cut thin shavings and always cut with the blade facing away from you.

With a metal rasp, shape the flat pieces so they curve up in the center and down at the ends. Use the rough side of the rasp for the shaping, the fine side of the rasp for finishing.

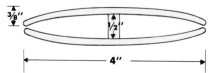

Use crosswise and lengthwise strokes as needed to approximate the shape shown above. After filing, sand lightly with very fine sandpaper.

For the center post, cut a ½-inch length of ¼-inch wooden dowel. Apply epoxy glue with a cotton-tipped swab to both cut ends and center the post between the sides.

Hold the shuttle together with a rubber band or a small clamp while the glue dries. To further secure the post, drive brads through both sides of the shuttle into the post.

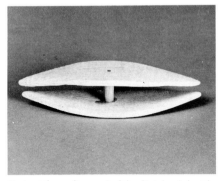

Protect the soft wood of the finished shuttle with two coats of clear shellac, sanding lightly between coats.

Weaving, Braiding, and Knotting
Openwork tablecloth

$ 🏷️30 🧍 🪔

Jay Duncan was born in Port McNicoll, Canada, and has spent most of her life in Toronto. She enjoys knitting, bread-dough sculpture, leather and copper work, and furniture refinishing, but her main interest is tatting. Jay teaches this old-fashioned craft to others, and makes tatted gifts for her family and friends.

This finely detailed formal tablecloth is decorative, rather than functional—you would want to remove it before dinner is served. The pattern is made with squares edged with triangles. You can make the cloth fit any size rectangular or square table by simply adding or subtracting squares.

This formal tablecloth is made up of squares joined with strips; the resulting square or rectangular cloth is edged with triangles. To make a rectangular cloth approximately 48 by 62 inches, you will need 130 squares (each 4¼ inches square) and 46 triangles (each 2½ inches deep).

Materials: 19 balls of ecru six-cord mercerized crochet cotton, size 20, and a tatting shuttle.

Directions
One triangular section of a square
Ring 1: 3 ds, P, 3 ds, P, 3 ds; close. Reverse work.
Chain 1: 6 ds, P, 6 ds, P, 6 ds. Reverse work.
Ring 2: 3 ds, join to second P of first ring, 3 ds, P, 3 ds; close. Reverse work.
Chain 2: 6 ds. Reverse work.
Ring 3: 3 ds, P, 3 ds, P, 3 ds; close. Reverse work.
Chain 3: 6 ds. Reverse work.
Ring 4: 3 ds, P, 3 ds, P, 3 ds; close. Reverse work.
Chain 4: 6 ds, join to last P of second chain, 6 ds, P, 6 ds. Reverse work.
Ring 5: 3 ds, join to second P of fourth ring, 3 ds, P, 3 ds; close. Reverse work.
Chain 5: 6 ds, P, 6 ds, P, 6 ds. Reverse work.

Ring 6: 3 ds, join to last P of previous ring, 3 ds, P, 3 ds; close. Reverse work.
Chain 6: 6 ds, P, 6 ds, P, 6 ds. Reverse work.
Ring 7: 3 ds, join to last P of previous ring, 3 ds, join to first P of first ring, 3 ds; close. Reverse work.
Chain 7: 6 ds. Reverse work.
Ring 8: 3 ds, join to first P of third ring, 3 ds, P, 3 ds; close. Reverse work.
Chain 8: 6 ds. Reverse work.
Ring 9: 3 ds, P, 3 ds, P, 3 ds; close. Reverse work.
Chain 9: 6 ds, join to second P of seventh chain, 6 ds, P, 6 ds. Reverse work.
Ring 10: 3 ds, join to second P of previous ring, 3 ds, P, 3 ds; close. Reverse work.
Chain 10: 6 ds. Reverse work.
Ring 11: 3 ds, P, 3 ds, P, 3 ds; close. Reverse work.
Chain 11: 6 ds. Reverse work.
Ring 12: 3 ds, P, 3 ds, P, 3 ds; close. Reverse work.
Chain 12: 6 ds, join to second P of previous chain, 6 ds, P, 6 ds. Reverse work.
Ring 13: 3 ds, join to second P of previous ring, 3 ds, P, 3 ds; close. Reverse work.

Chain 13: 6 ds. Reverse work.
Ring 14: 3 ds, P, 3 ds, P, 3 ds; close. Reverse work.
Chain 14: 6 ds. Reverse work.
Ring 15: 3 ds, P, 3 ds, P, 3 ds; close. Reverse work.
Chain 15: 6 ds, join to second P of previous chain, 6 ds, join to first P of chain 6, 6 ds. Reverse work.
Ring 16: 3 ds, join to second P of previous ring, 3 ds, P, 3 ds; close. Reverse work.
Chain 16: 6 ds, join to first P of previous chain, 6 ds, P, 6 ds. Reverse work.
Ring 17: 3 ds, join to second P of previous ring, 3 ds, P, 3 ds; close. Reverse work.

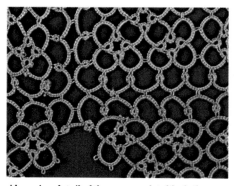

Above is a detail of the openwork tablecloth shown top left.

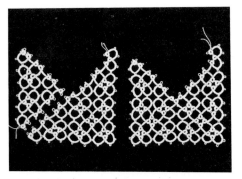

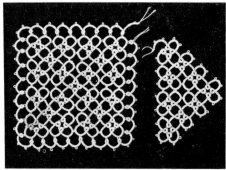

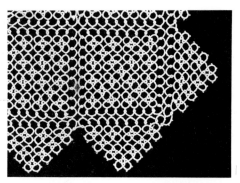

1: Each square of the tablecloth is made of four triangles. At left, half a square is shown with the third triangle worked separately for demonstration purposes. On the right, the third triangle was joined to the first two as it was worked, as would be the case if you were making the square.

2: When a square is completed, a joining strip—a round of curved chains and rings attached to the outer picots of the square—is added. One of the triangles that form the edging is shown at the right, as it looks before the joining strip that will be worked along one side of it is added.

3: The squares and triangles are joined in turn to neighboring pieces with the joining strips as the strips are made. You can make the squares and triangles separately; then use joining strips to connect the pieces when you have a sufficient number.

Chain 17: 6 ds, P, 6 ds, P, 6 ds. Reverse work.

Ring 18: 3 ds, join to second P of previous ring, 3 ds, join to first P of first ring, 3 ds; close. Reverse work.

Chain 18: 6 ds. Reverse work.

Ring 19: 3 ds, join to second P of previous ring, 3 ds, P, 3 ds; close. Reverse work.

Chain 19: 6 ds. Reverse work.

Ring 20: 3 ds, P, 3 ds, P, 3 ds; close. Reverse work.

Chain 20: 6 ds, join to second P of previous chain, 6 ds, P, 6 ds. Reverse work.

Ring 21: 3 ds, join to second P of previous ring, 3 ds, P, 3 ds; close. Reverse work.

Chain 21: 6 ds, P, 6 ds, P, 6 ds. Reverse work.

Ring 22: 3 ds, join to second P of previous ring, 3 ds, P, 3 ds; close.

This triangle is one quarter of one square. Repeat the preceding directions for the remaining three triangles, joining each triangle to the others until the square is completed (photograph 1). Tie the ends and cut off.

Joining the edging to the completed square (photograph 2)

Ring 1: 3 ds, join to first P of square, 3 ds; close. Reverse work.

Chain 1: 6 ds, P, 6 ds. Reverse work.

Ring 2: 3 ds, join to second P of square, 3 ds; close. Reverse work.

Chain 2: 6 ds, P, 6 ds. Reverse work.

Ring 3: 3 ds, join to third P of square. 3 ds; close.

Continue in this sequence to the corner.

At the corner: Chain (6 ds, P, 6 ds, P, 6 ds); repeat sequence of rings and chains to next corner.

Make as many squares as necessary to fit your table, joining each square in turn to the joining edge of the adjacent square.

The first triangle of the finishing edge

Chain 1: 6 ds, P, 6 ds, P, 6 ds. Reverse work.

Ring 1: 3 ds, join to second P of previous chain, 3 ds, P, 3 ds; close. Reverse work.

Chain 2: 6 ds, P, 6 ds, P, 6 ds. Reverse work.

Ring 2: 3 ds, join to second P of previous ring, 3 ds, join to first P of first ring, 3 ds; close. Reverse work.

Chain 3: 6 ds. Reverse work.

Ring 3: 3 ds, join to second P of previous ring, 3 ds, P, 3 ds; close. Reverse work.

Chain 4: 6 ds, P, 6 ds, P, 6 ds. Reverse work.

Ring 4: 3 ds, join to second P of previous ring, 3 ds, join to first P of first ring, 3 ds; close. Reverse work.

Chain 5: 6 ds. Reverse work.

Ring 5: 3 ds, join to second P of previous ring, 3 ds, P, 3 ds; close. Reverse work.

Chain 6: 6 ds, P, 6 ds, P, 6 ds. Reverse work.

Ring 6: 3 ds, join to second P of previous ring, 3 ds, join to first P of first ring, 3 ds; close. Reverse work.

Chain 7: 6 ds. Reverse work.

Ring 7: 3 ds, join to second P of previous ring, 3 ds, P, 3 ds; close. Reverse work.

Chain 8: 6 ds, P, 6 ds, P, 6 ds. Reverse work.

Ring 8: 3 ds, join to second P of previous ring, 3 ds, join to first P of first ring, 3 ds; close.

Continue on second side of triangle; tie ends and cut off.

To join triangle to edge of square, use same joining edge technique used for joining squares, except for the corners and for joining the triangles to each other.

Corners and joinings of triangles

Chain 1: 6 ds, join to last P of square, 6 ds, P, 6 ds. Reverse work.

Ring 1: 3 ds, join to second P of edge of triangle, 3 ds; close. Reverse work.

Chain 2: 6 ds. Reverse work.

Ring 2: 3 ds, join to first P of next triangle, 3 ds; close. Reverse work.

Chain 3: 6 ds, join to second P of previous ring, 6 ds, join to second P of joining edge of next square. Reverse work.

Ring 3: 3 ds, join to second P of triangle, 3 ds; close.

Continue to corner of tablecloth. Complete joining triangles to squares. Reverse work.

Chain 1: 6 ds, P, 6 ds, P, 6 ds. Reverse work.

Ring 1: 3 ds, join to next triangle, 3 ds; close. Reverse work.

Chain 2: 6 ds, join to second P of joining edge of triangle, 6 ds, join to corner of square, 6 ds. Reverse work.

Ring 2: 3 ds, join to triangle, 3 ds; close.

Continue until edge is complete. Join to beginning of edging; tie the ends and cut off.

For related crafts and entries, see "Granny Squares" and "Lace."